Small Quilts with
Vintage Charm

8 Projects to Decorate Your Home

Jo Morton

C&T PUBLISHING

Text © 2005 Jo Morton

Artwork © 2005 C&T Publishing, Inc.

Publisher: Amy Marson

Editorial Director: Gailen Runge

Acquisitions Editor: Jan Grigsby

Editor: Lynn Koolish

Technical Editors: Elin Thomas, Joyce Lytle, and Cynthia Keyes Hilton

Copyeditor/Proofreader: Wordfirm,Inc.

Cover Designer: Kristy A. Konitzer

Design Director/Book Designer: Kristy A. Konitzer

Illustrator: Richard Sheppard

Production Assistant: Tim Manibusan

Photography: Luke Mulks, unless otherwise noted

Published by C&T Publishing, Inc., P.O. Box 1456, Lafayette, CA 94549

Front cover: Photo by Diane Pedersen

Back cover: Concentric Log Cabin, and Log Cabin with Dogtooth Border

Library of Congress Cataloging-in-Publication Data

Morton, Mary Jo Gress

  Small quilts with vintage charm : 8 projects to decorate your home / Jo Morton.

    p. cm.

  Includes index.

  ISBN 1-57120-270-6 (paper trade)

  1. Quilting--Patterns. 2. Patchwork--Patterns. 3. Miniature quilts. I. Title.

TT835.M6895 2005

746.46'041--dc22

2004020814

Printed in China

10 9 8 7 6 5 4 3 2 1

Dedication

This book is dedicated to my mother, Mary Gress, who has always believed in me and encouraged me. She has also insisted on having good tools to do good work. My mother is an excellent seamstress, knitter, and crocheter. She is a perfectionist in her sewing, and she has shared that virtue with me.

By the way, I did teach her to quilt in 1982. She made lovely hand-quilting stitches. When we both worked on the same quilt, you couldn't tell who had quilted what part. She still sews down bindings for me when I need her help.

Table of Contents

Acknowledgments

First to my husband, Russ, for his love and support and for respecting all the time I need for my work. He has shared in making many a meal, has done many "honey, can you please do this for me" chores, and is proud of my accomplishments. We celebrate deadlines by trips to Omaha for a great meal out.

To my friend Donna Stratker, who happens to be my sister-in-law (Russ's sister): thank you for introducing me to quilting in 1979. We've attended lots of classes and outings together. I'm looking forward to more.

I would like to thank my friends from the quilt guild in Waterloo, Nebraska (about 75 miles from home), to which I belonged in the early 1980s. Through their special friendships, they guided, mentored, and encouraged me. I treasure those times and friendships. We are still friends, and I always look forward to our time together. You know who you are.

Living with Small Quilts

In the spirit of renewing the past, I design and make small quilts to help fulfill my passion for living with the old or with the new made to look old. It is a lifestyle—not a trendy choice—that I follow. I've found my own way of living with these small quilts, as well as interesting ways to enjoy them. This is what I want to share with you.

I live in a small bungalow from the 1930s with my husband, Russ, and two kitties, Socks and Tigger. Every wall in our home is broken up with windows or doors, so we don't have large walls to feature a big quilt like you might see in books and magazines. In addition, because we live with kitties, and I don't want to provide them with quilts for napping, we use a washable bedspread, rather than a quilt, on our bed.

So, what do I do with my small quilts? Everyone knows what to do with a bed-sized quilt or a wallhanging, but what to do with the others? Here are some of my suggestions for using and displaying a small-quilt collection.

Photo by Mark Jewell

Protect Your Quilts

When displaying quilts, be sure to keep them out of direct sunlight to minimize fading. You may want to rotate your quilt display so no one quilt is over-exposed.

Displaying Quilts

ON THE WALL

The normal thought for what to do with smaller quilts is to hang them on a wall. These are often called wallhangings. I don't think of my quilts just as wallhangings; instead, I think of them as small quilts that sometimes get used as wallhangings but that can also be displayed in other ways in our home.

I am frequently asked how I hang my quilts. Over the years, I tried several methods that involved a typical quilt sleeve, but I had never found a hanging method that I liked. Now, instead of a sleeve, I use sturdy straight pins in the top corners and, if needed, one or two more pins across the top of the quilt. This method works nicely on wallboard and can be used with care on plaster walls.

Instead of hanging one quilt on a wall, try hanging a group of doll-sized quilts to make a nice display.

OVER A CHAIR OR SOFA

Displaying a quilt over the back of a chair or sofa is another easy use for small quilts. For a smaller-sized quilt used in this manner, you may need to fold it carefully for it to look its best.

IN A CUPBOARD AND MORE

Decorating books and magazines often show bed-sized quilts folded and stacked in an open cupboard or pie safe. They look great, don't they?

The problem with this type of display for small quilts is that they don't show off nicely when folded, and folding causes them to crease. The solution is to fold the small quilts over a few layers of cotton batting as padding, which creates a nice rounded fold and adds depth to a stack of smaller-sized quilts.

You can also use the batting idea for small doll quilts folded and stacked on a shelf or in a trunk, suitcase, or baby buggy. Adjust the batting according to your quilt sizes. If you don't have any trunks or baby buggies for displaying your small treasures, perhaps it is time for a little antiquing! While on these antiquing trips, look for doll cradles, doll beds, or small chairs. These items go nicely with dolls or bears from your collection or your childhood.

ON A TABLE

Use a small quilt under a lamp to protect the painted surface or wood finish of a table or cupboard. This idea also adds color and texture to a decorative setting. Think of the number of times decorating shows on television mention "texture." A small quilt can add softness between the hard surfaces of the table and lamp.

Photo by Mark Jewell

Use a small quilt as the unifying texture for a setting. Place a quilt under a basket, folk-art carvings, a wooden or pottery bowl, or any number of treasures you have collected. When using small quilts in this manner, you should use what I call "Plain Jane quilts," or quilts that don't compete with the items you are grouping together. Instead, these quilts enhance the setting. You can determine what works best by auditioning your quilts for the setting—the right quilt will speak to you.

ON THE DINING ROOM TABLE

A dining room table is a wonderful place to display quilts for seasonal or nonseasonal decor. Look for (or make) a woven cotton runner in your preferred colors, and use it as the foundation for your decor. Layer a quilt on top of the runner. If the quilt is square, consider featuring it on point.

Photo by Mark Jewell

Sometimes I place one of my rectangular quilts on the woven runner, with the ends of the runner protruding from under the quilt. Visually, the runner adds length to the setting. I then add a favorite piece of pottery, wooden bowl, basket, or flower arrangement and some candles.

Try using two or more small quilts over the woven runner on your table before adding accessories. The possibilities are endless.

WATCH THOSE CANDLES

If you eat at a table you display your quilts on, be sure to remove the quilt before meals. When using candles near your quilts, make sure to use dripless candles or candleholders with bases to catch drips. Consider various candleholder solutions so you do not get candle wax on your quilts.

BASKETS

Quite a few years ago, I purchased a wonderful gathering basket that had been painted mustard and distressed to look old. When I got home and placed the basket on top of the cupboard in our dining room, no one could see the basket because the top of the cupboard was recessed. I tipped the basket on its side, and loved the look of it sitting that way, but then the icky gray interior showed. What to do? I went to the jelly cupboard, sorted through my smaller quilts, and found a Log Cabin quilt that fit perfectly in the bottom of the basket. The quilt simply lies in the basket and adds subtle color and texture on top of our dining room cupboard. Using this Plain Jane quilt was a nice solution to my dilemma.

Photo by Jo Morton

MORE DISPLAY IDEAS

A few years ago, I found a small ladder, about five feet tall, in a central Missouri antique shop. I display folded quilts and handwoven blankets on this ladder in our family room. If you can't find an old ladder, look for a newly made ladder in a country store or at a craft show. You may even get lucky on your excursion and drive by a quilt shop, where you can find more fabric for your collection!

PREVENTING STAINS

Place a couple of layers of washed, unbleached muslin over the ladder rungs before hanging your quilt. Remember, moisture in wood can seep and cause permanent stains on textiles.

CONSERVATION FRAMING

Framing is a good preservation technique for both new and old textiles. It is a wonderful way to show-case a special small quilt or antique textile. A professional framer can offer many options. Here are some things to think about:

❋ Select a frame in a color and style to comple-ment the quilt and your home.

❋ Select an acid-free mat board (also called museum board) in a color or shade that enhances the quilt. You also may wish to consider a linen mat.

In our all-too-busy lives, machine quilting is replac-ing hand quilting. But you can hand quilt small quilts in a short time. These smaller quilts, properly framed, produce wonderful pieces of art for your home and preserve the time-honored tradition of hand quilting.

You should refold your quilts at least a few times a year. Refold them in the opposite direction so the creases do not become permanent. When you refold your quilts, be sure to wash the white cotton liner sheets or muslin to keep your storage area clean.

Fold your quilts right side out, because the inside of a fold creases fabric the worst. For smaller quilts, fold three or four similarly sized quilts together, right side out. The quilts themselves act as the padding, so there are no hard creases from folding.

When you refold your quilts, rotate them so the inside quilt is now on the outside, and be sure to refold them in the opposite direction. This change creates a thicker fold for the quilts and a nice appearance on the edge of the shelf.

Photo by Mark Jewell

Storage

It is important to store your quilts with conservation and preservation in mind. Quilts are often stored on wooden shelves in closets or cupboards or in wooden blanket chests. It is always important to ensure that the wood does not touch your quilts directly, because seepage from the wood can stain textiles. Seal new wood with polyurethane varnish. Be sure to line shelves and blanket chests with washed, white cotton sheets or new, washed, unbleached muslin.

Photo by Mark Jewell

Fabric for vintage-looking quilt

Choosing and Using Fabric

Even I call my quilts "scrap quilts." What a misnomer! My quilts are scrappy in the sense that I use what I have on hand, but they are composed of carefully selected pieces of fabric, not scraps pulled out of a bag and assembled without thought to color or value. For me to make a scrappy quilt, I must control the fabrics and not work randomly.

Choosing fabric carefully is the key to making new quilts that look old. We cannot duplicate or replicate an antique quilt exactly, because different dyes are used to produce today's fabrics, but we can achieve the look and feel of an old quilt.

In 1985, when I decided to attempt my first new quilt that looked old, I found a picture of a scrappy Nine-Patch crib quilt in a 1983 *Country Living* magazine. I used that quilt as a model for the value and contrast I wanted. You don't need to imitate an exact picture of a quilt—just look for a quilt that has a feeling you like. When I saw that picture, I was intrigued by the low contrast, the fabrics, and how it all came together to make a quilt I would love to own.

Not all antique quilts, by which I mean quilts made before 1900, are wonderful (some might even be called homely). But homeliness can be part of the charm of antique doll-, crib-, and bed-sized quilts.

Buying Fabric

Finding fabrics that add interest to a quilt can be a challenge. Some antique quilts contain what I call "icky fabrics," which add life and action to the completed quilt. An icky fabric is an unusual print or color that adds interest and makes me wonder why it is there. Icky fabrics can include stripes, plaids, squiggly prints, or medium- to large-scale prints that cut up wonderfully and are in colors that don't match the quilt.

A lot of quilters tend to buy pretty fabrics and small tone-on-tone prints that read solid. Where is the spark in those? Buy different shades and hues of many colors to make a quilt work. Many shades of red—pink red, brick red, blue red, cranberry red, wine red, and dark blood red—in different prints are far more interesting than the same red, which only ends up reading the same. Look for multicolored prints that cut up well and that add more interest to your block, setting, and quilt than tone-on-tone prints do. Avoid solid fabric; all it does is read flat.

Buy a variety of small, medium, and large prints, paisleys, geometrics, plaids, checks, and stripes. Did I miss anything? To re-create old quilts, you will need busy prints that have life, keep your eye moving across a quilt, and hold your interest. For effective scrap quilts, you must learn to buy a wide range of colors, not just your favorites.

WHICH FABRIC FIRST?

You may have been told to buy your border fabric first, then add fabrics in colors that appear in the border fabric. I rarely do that anymore. Instead, I suggest first making blocks that you like in fabrics that appeal to you. Then accept the challenge of finding the right fabric for the setting and borders. I think you end up with a better quilt using this method.

Sometimes, however, a particular fabric is the starting point for a quilt (notice I didn't say it had to be used for the border). This fabric may be the setting fabric, or you might use it in some or all of the blocks. This scenario exemplifies the first rule of quilting: there are no rules.

For me, regardless of the order, the fabric choices are the most important part of the quilt.

HOW MUCH FABRIC TO BUY?

Buy at least a fat quarter or bundles of them. A half yard is usually better because it folds nicely and is easier to store than smaller cuts. I buy many half-yard cuts because making scrappy quilts requires lots of choices and a variety of different shades, patterns, and hues.

If I like the fabric, I purchase a full yard (remember the small size in which I tend to work). From there, it depends on my mood. For backgrounds, I buy $1\frac{1}{2}$ to 2 yards; for borders and settings, 2 to 3 yards. If I really, really love a fabric, I may purchase 5 or 6 yards—3 yards to put away in the closet for later use and 3 yards for immediate use. I buy fabric for my fabric collection—when I get inspired to start a quilt, I begin with what I have on my shelves; most of the time, I can make my quilt from the fabric in my collection and don't have to go shopping. When you live 50 miles from the nearest quilt shop, as I do, having fabric on hand allows you to create when inspiration strikes.

I store extra fabric in the closet. In that closet, I keep the larger cuts separate from the smaller cuts, because it is easier to work with the $\frac{1}{2}$- to 1-yard cuts during block assembly. I then go to the closet for setting and border fabrics.

BACKING

Purchase backing fabric *after* your quilt top is complete so you can select a fabric that complements the front of the quilt. Using fabric that you don't want anymore does a disservice to the quilt top. Remember, the two pieces will be stitched together forever; therefore, they need to be compatible and interesting.

Preparing Fabric

I prewash all my fabric. Whether I'm sewing by hand or machine, I prefer the way prewashed fabric handles during piecing and appliquéing.

Use soap and the permanent press or gentle wash cycle on your washer, toss the fabric in the dryer, remove it when it is almost dry (don't overdry, or you will set in wrinkles), fold it immediately, and place it on the shelf. Press the fabric when you are ready to use it in a project.

The fabric weave will tighten up during prewashing and drying, making the fabric easier to handle and less likely to ravel. Washing also gives it a better hand.

Many shades of red: burgundy, wine, brick, blood red, blue red, orange red, pink red

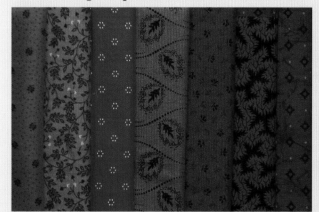

Browns: chocolate, walnut

Blacks

Rusts (madder family)

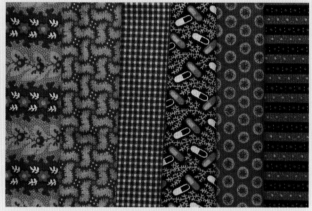

Color

To help you select colors for your quilt project, look at pictures of quilts with colors you like. Take note of the shades of the colors used. Is there more than one shade or hue of a color? For my quilts, I tend to prefer some grayed tones of various colors, rather than pure or bright tones, even though the original antique fabrics may have been brighter. I believe that using toned-down colors enhances the aged appearance.

I constantly look for certain color families to add to my collection, but I also pay attention to the design of the fabric for an antique feel. Don't forget to look for multicolored pieces, too. The fabrics on these pages are some of my favorites.

Auditioning Fabrics

Now that you have purchased and prepared your fabric, there are several ways to select the specific fabrics before you start your quilt.

Begin with a picture of a quilt you like or whose colors you want to imitate. I recommend keeping scrapbooks with pictures of quilts for border ideas, settings, blocks, and colors. These pictures are a good starting point—very few of us can design from scratch.

Here's my suggestion for auditioning fabric:

Start by placing your fabrics on the table as you select them. If you like what you see, place the fabrics on the floor to get some distance.

Gold shades

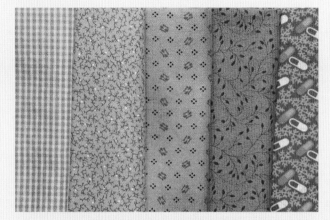

For backgrounds: tan shades, taupe shades, sometimes gray shades, and light browns in a variety of patterns

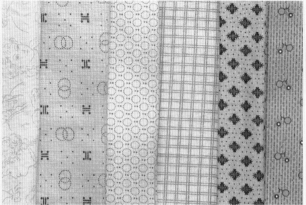

Greens: olive drab, poison (yellow green), sage

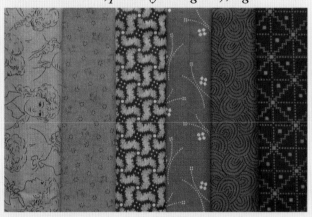

Eggplant

Use a reducing glass to look at the fabrics from even farther away so that you can see how they will read in a quilt across a room. Squint at the fabrics. Rearrange them and look through the reducing glass again. All too often, I see people attempting to select fabrics that are only 12 to 18 inches from their nose, and then they wonder why they don't like their quilt when it is hanging on the wall across the room. We know why—they haven't auditioned the fabrics from afar. You need to see how the fabrics will read.

Leave the fabrics on the floor for a few days, walking around or over them while you work on other projects. Add and subtract fabrics as you pass by until you are satisfied with your choices. It is important to make good fabric choices at this point, because once you begin piecing, it is harder to make changes.

Starting to Work

When you are happy with the selected fabrics, pin the potential setting fabric to your design wall. Next, fold the potential border fabric to the desired width and pin it to the edge of the setting fabric. Then begin making the blocks. This way, you can see how the whole quilt reads as you go. It also allows you to make changes before cutting into the bigger pieces of fabric for the setting or border. Try pinning up two different setting fabrics to decide which works best. Use the same method for the borders—pin up two or more different choices, and then decide.

General Instructions

Fabric

I recommend 100% cotton fabrics purchased from a quilt shop. You want good-quality material for the quilt you will be spending hours making. (Refer to pages 10–11 for more suggestions for choosing and buying fabric.)

Thread

Use 100% cotton thread in various weights.

❀ For hand or machine piecing, use a 50/3-or 60/2-weight thread.

❀ For hand appliqué, use a 50/3- or 60/2-weight thread, depending on the project.

❀ For hand quilting, use a heavier 40/3-weight.

Remember that the *bigger* the number, the *finer* the thread. The 50-weight thread varies from brand to brand, so select the one that works best for you and your machine.

I like to use Mettler color #514 (a tan to light brown shade) for most of my hand quilting, because it is perfect for my darker light fabrics and doesn't create white sparkling stitches, as a color like ecru would. This color shade also adds the illusion of a patina to my quilts. However, you may want to use black quilting thread on some dark projects.

Thread for quilting

Batting

In most of my quilts, I have used 100% cotton Mountain Mist Blue Ribbon batting. Over the years, I have tried other battings, but I keep returning to Mountain Mist Blue Ribbon. I like the way my quilts look with this batting when hand or machine quilted. In addition, this batting, which gives the flat look and feel of an antique quilt, drapes nicely and washes beautifully.

Accuracy

Basic quiltmaking skills, such as using an accurate scant 1/4" seam allowance, exact rotary cutting, and precise measuring, are absolutely necessary for these smaller-scale quilts to go together nicely.

ACCURATE CUTTING

To cut the pieces for these smaller projects, you need a good ruler with a 1/8" grid. I suggest the following ruler sizes.

For cutting out and squaring units and blocks:

❀ A 4" x 4" or 6" x 6" that has a corner section with a 1/8" grid, or

❀ A 4" x 8" that is entirely covered with a 1/8" grid

For cutting borders:

❀ A 6" x 12", 6" x 18", or 6" x 24"

NON-SLIP RULERS

Make your rulers non-slip by applying non-slip dots or InvisiGrip.

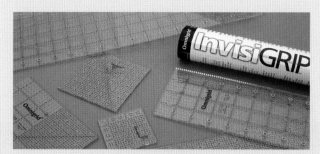

Recommended rulers

For consistently accurate cutting:

❀ Be sure the edges and corners of your rulers are sharp and the lines easy to read, not worn off.

❀ Measure the fabric using the grid lines on the ruler. **Do not** use the lines on your cutting mat.

❀ When cutting your fabric, hold the ruler carefully. If the ruler slips, your piece will not be the correct size and your piecing will be off.

Sometimes, due to the size of the blocks in my quilts, I end up with interesting measurements such as $1/16$". I eyeball the $1/16$" measurement evenly spaced between the $1/8$" marks on most rulers.

ACCURATE SEWING

Use a $1/4$" foot on your sewing machine to achieve a consistently accurate scant $1/4$" seam allowance. Why scant? If you sew exactly on the $1/4$" line, some of the fabric will be taken up by the fold after pressing, and the block will shrink a bit. This problem, which can be compounded if you have many seams, will create a discrepancy in the finished block size. Precision is especially important when making small quilts.

I piece my blocks with a Pfaff 2040, with the dual feed mechanism engaged. Before I owned this machine, I used a walking foot for piecing so that my seams would be straight and not get off track when I sewed over seam intersections (diagonal seams are the worst).

FABRIC GRAIN

Understanding fabric grain is important for accurate piecing.

❀ Straight of grain is either the lengthwise or crosswise of the fabric.

❀ Lengthwise grain has little or no give to it. Crosswise grain has a slight give.

❀ Keeping the straight of grain on the outside edges of your quilt blocks is important in keeping your work accurate.

❀ Use the straight of grain to your advantage in your quiltmaking. Doing so will make assembling your projects a pleasure. Use the lengthwise grain on borders and sashings, unless you want the design of the fabric to run in a different direction.

CUTTING TRIANGLES

Half-square triangles have a bias edge on the long side of the triangle. The straight of grain is on the two short sides. Half-squared triangles are cut diagonally through a square.

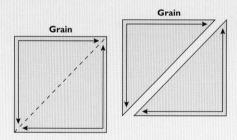

Cutting half-square triangles

When a square is cut twice diagonally, it results in quarter-square triangles, which have the bias edges on the short sides of the triangle. The straight of grain is on the long side of the triangle.

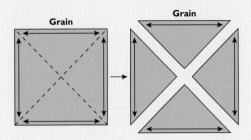

Cutting quarter-square triangles

Remember that you want the straight of grain on the outside of your quilt blocks, so always follow the project directions when cutting your triangles.

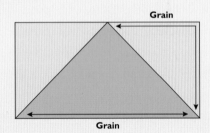

Keep straight of grain on outside edges of blocks.

KEEPING IT STRAIGHT

Do your Log Cabin blocks wave at you? If so, think about whether you cut your strips on the lengthwise or crosswise grain of the fabric. From now on, always cut the strips on the lengthwise grain of the fabric, *unless you are cutting to take advantage of the directional design of a fabric. This requirement is also a good reason to purchase half-yard cuts of fabric so that you have at least 18" lengthwise strips for piecing.*

Rit Tan Dyeing

I love the way Rit #16 tan dye mellows out fabric—it takes the edge off, so the fabric doesn't look so new, and it gets rid of the white in designs. In quilts that are made to look old, white areas jump out at me like dots and distract me from the overall effect. The white bothers my eyes; but this preference may be a personal thing, and whites may not affect you in the same way.

My method for Rit tan dyeing works in our Nebraska City water; your results may vary.

One bottle of Rit #16 tan dye will overdye about 8 yards of fabric (less if you are overdyeing dark fabrics, more if you are overdyeing light fabrics). You can mix light and dark fabrics in the process. Be sure to prewash your fabric to remove the sizing so the dye is accepted more evenly. I prefer the color I get with the Rit liquid rather than the Rit powder, which seems to have a more pink-tan shade.

1. The fabrics to be dyed must be evenly wet before dyeing. Soak them in water while the washer is filling.

2. Using the hot/warm setting on your washing machine, fill it with hot water. Shake the dye bottle well and add the liquid dye before the washer begins to agitate.

3. Squeeze out the excess water from the fabric and add the darker fabrics first, then the lighter fabrics. Add the fabric while the washer agitates, making sure to unfold your fabric as you put it in the washer. Fabric that is folded or wadded up won't dye evenly.

4. Let the washing machine go through all its cycles.

5. Put the fabric in the dryer. Take it out before it is completely dry and fold it so the wrinkles don't get set. Press the fabric before cutting.

Rit dye is *not* permanent, no matter what you do, even if you add salt or vinegar to set it. Fabric dyed with Rit will fade on the shelf along the fold line, but usually only after several years. If your stored fabric does fade, simply cut around the fade line if it bothers you; sometimes I leave the lighter area for an interesting look.

I recommend washing dark clothes or towels (or something with bleach) after dyeing to make sure all the dye is gone from your washer. The dye may slightly darken the tub and agitator, but I don't mind that. The mellow look of my quilts is most important to me, and no one but me sees the inside of my washer.

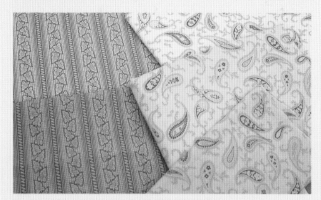

Before and after dyeing; note that different batches will not be identical

Clipping Trick

Use this "trick" for block piecing, block settings, and border piecing. It will make your seam intersections much less bulky, which will make it easier to hand or machine quilt your project.

1. Clip up to the seam line 1/4" on *each* side of the seam intersection (clips will be 1/2" apart). Clip each seam allowance separately to avoid cutting through the stitching.

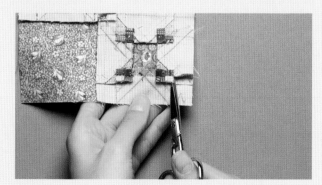

Clip seam allowances.

2. Press the seam allowances in the direction they naturally lie to reduce the bulk of the layers. Press the center intersection open.

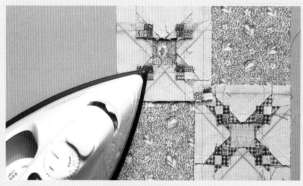

Press seam allowances.

3. See how nice and flat your block lies?

Pressed block

Single-Thickness Binding

Use a single-thickness binding on your smaller quilts; a double-thickness binding is too heavy for most small quilts and can contribute to a wavy edge. This is important for the quilt to hang nicely on the wall.

MAKE THE BINDING

1. Cut binding strips 1 1/8" wide on the crossgrain of the fabric (from selvage to selvage). Take advantage of the slight give in the grain of the fabric, which will make the binding process easier.

2. Sew the short ends together, using a diagonal seam, to make one piece long enough to go around your quilt. Allow about 8"–10" excess to join the ends. To sew the diagonal seam, place the square ends of 2 pieces at a right angle, slightly overlapping the ends. With right sides together, sew the seam and then backstitch at both ends.

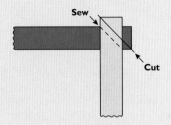

Sew seam and backstitch.

3. Press the seam(s) open.

Press open.

SEW THE BINDING TO THE QUILT

1. With right sides together, align a raw edge of the binding with the raw edge of your quilt. Sew using a ¼" seam allowance and leave about 3"–4" of binding free at the beginning.

2. To miter the corner, stop ¼" from the edge of the quilt and backstitch.

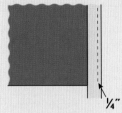

Stop ¼" from the edge.

3. With the needle down, rotate the quilt ¼ turn. Make sure your quilt doesn't move, move the needle

to the up position, and then fold up the binding at a 45° angle.

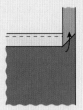

Fold up at 45° angle.

4. Fold the binding back down over the first fold, creating a 90° corner that is even with the top raw edge of the quilt and aligned with the side raw edge of the quilt.

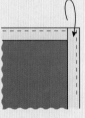

Fold down.

5. Begin with a backstitch to secure the end, and sew using a ¼" seam allowance to the next corner.

6. Repeat Steps 2 through 5 at each corner. Stop sewing about 5" or 6" from the start.

JOIN THE ENDS OF THE BINDING

1. Fold the bottom binding strip toward the center of the quilt at a 45° angle.

2. Fold the top binding strip toward the edge of the quilt at a 45° angle, leaving about an ⅛" gap between the folds. Press.

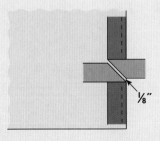

Leave ⅛" between the folds.

3. Pin the folds together, sew in the crease, and backstitch at both ends of the seam.

4. Trim excess binding strips, leaving a ¼" seam allowance. Press the seam open. Finish sewing the binding in place.

5. Trim the excess batting and backing.

6. Fold the binding to the back, turn under the raw edge ¼", and pin in place. Miter the corners when turning to the back.

7. Blindstitch or slipstitch the binding on the back of the quilt. Use close, small stitches to conceal the machine stitching, but don't stitch through to the front of the quilt. Use 3 to 4 extra stitches on the folds of the mitered corners to hold them in place.

Binding Tips

1. Leave a ⅛" gap when you join the ends of the binding so your binding will lie flat and you won't have to worry about easing in any excess.
2. Use a walking foot to attach the binding to help prevent the edges from stretching.

Needle-turn Appliqué

1. For templates, use freezer paper, plastic template material, self-adhesive laminating paper, or your favorite material. Trace the appliqué shape onto the selected template material. Cut out the shape with paper-cutting scissors.

2. Use a Clover marking pen (fine white, item #517) or a mechanical pencil (0.9mm) to draw around the template(s). You will need more than one marking tool for various colors of fabrics.

Draw around template.

3. Use a good sharp pair of fabric scissors (5" is a nice size) to trim the excess fabric, leaving approximately a 3/16" or a fat ⅛" turn-under allowance. Pin or thread baste the appliqué pieces onto the background fabric.

4. Thread your needle with 18" of matching or blending thread. Knot the end. I like to use needles such as John James 11 sharps or Jeana Kimball's 10 straws, along with a good sturdy needle threader. Needle threaders are handy for needles with small eyes, not to mention kinder to aging eyes.

5. Begin to appliqué along a flat edge of the appliqué piece. Finger-press a short area, about ½" or so, along the marked line.

6. Hold the pressed area in place with your non-sewing hand, and come up from the background, behind the appliqué piece. Bring your needle out the folded edge. Bury the knot in the fold; don't leave knots on the back.

7. Put the needle into the background, as close as possible to where the thread came out from the fold. Take about a 1/16" stitch, coming up through the edge of the appliqué. Barely catch the folded edge of the appliqué piece so the thread will not be seen.

8. After a few stitches, use your needle (or a wetted, round wooden toothpick) to gently fold and smooth under the turn-under allowance. Turn under just enough fabric for a stitch or two. Make sure the allowance is smooth so you won't have points where you don't want them. Avoid touching the raw edge of the fabric with your needle because it can cause fraying.

INNER POINTS

1. When you come to an inside point and cannot turn under the fabric any more, use your small, sharp embroidery scissors to carefully clip to the point.

2. Use your needle to turn under the fabric to the point.

3. Take smaller stitches, and sew to the point.

Sew to point using smaller stitches.

4. When you reach the point, turn under the allowance on the other side and smooth it with your needle. Make sure all the threads are turned under, then take an extra stitch in the inside point and continue up the other side. Gradually increase your stitch length from 1/16" to 1/8".

Continue on other side of point.

OUTER POINTS

1. For a sharp outer point, stitch to the point and fold under the end at a 90° angle. Take a stitch to secure.

Stitch to secure point.

2. Use your needle to turn under the other side. Sweep the fabric under with your needle or a toothpick.

Sweep fabric under.

3. Give the thread a tug to pull out the point. Hold the folded fabric down with your thumb and continue with small appliqué stitches.

TRIMMING

Carefully trim excess fabric at the point where you turn it under to avoid bulk that can cause a rounded point or lump.

ENDING OFF

1. After stitching the shape in place, insert the needle next to the appliqué edge and pull the thread to the back.

2. Wrap the thread around the needle twice, hold the needle down next to the fabric, and pull your needle and thread through the loops to create a knot just on top of the fabric.

3. Insert your needle where the thread came out, then bury the knot between the background fabric and the appliqué fabric.

4. Clip your thread next to the fabric.

Finished appliqué

I don't cut away any of the background fabric behind the appliqué. In the antique quilts I have examined, the fabric was left in place, helping keep the blocks more stable.

Washing Quilts

Taking good care of your quilts (whether large or small) will extend their lives so you can enjoy them for years to come. Wash only when (and if) absolutely necessary. To help extend the time between washing, you can tumble your quilts in a dryer set on air fluff (no heat). Add a damp towel to help collect dust and pet hair.

1. Use Orvus or other mild soap intended for washing quilts and set your washer to a medium-temperature water setting (my machine is on the cooler side).

2. Soak your quilt in the washing machine for about ten minutes. Use your hands to squish the quilt a few times, then soak a bit longer. Do not agitate.

3. Change the machine setting to drain out the soapy water.

4. Refill the machine with medium to cool water. Squish the quilt again with your hands to help remove the soapy water.

5. Spin out the rinse water.

6. Refill the machine one more time with medium to cool water to be sure all the soap is removed; squish the quilt with your hands again.

7. Spin out the rinse water and then let the washer spin a bit longer to help remove excess water from the quilt.

8. Carefully remove the quilt. Put it in the dryer for only a few minutes to help soften the wrinkles.

9. Here is the best part: get out your electric blanket. Spread it on the carpet or bed, cover it with a clean white sheet, and turn it on high.

10. Spread your quilt over the electric blanket and smooth out any wrinkles. You can almost block your quilt by lightly pulling on the edges.

11. Let the quilt dry for a couple of hours and check it. If it feels pretty dry, turn it over and dry from the other side for as long as it takes (probably a couple more hours). If your quilt is larger than the electric blanket, you may need to move it around over the electric blanket to get all the areas dried.

When you're done, you will have a nice, flat quilt. Because you've done all your drying inside, you don't have to worry about birds flying overhead or creases from a clothesline. This method is also much faster than having fans move air over a quilt. That's a very good thing.

Sarah's Album Cross

Inspired by a bed-sized quilt from the 1840s, I scaled the original block down to make this enchanting wall quilt, which is one of my favorites—and I am not a blue person. I have decided it ranks among my favorites because it has lots of browns, rusts/reds, and caramel tans.

The Album Cross block is perfect for playing with your fabric collection or perhaps adding to it. About two-thirds of the blocks in the quilt are made using only three fabrics. For the remaining one-third, I made the blocks scrappier but kept them within one color family.

This quilt grew beyond my initial plan of making 25 blocks, which just didn't make enough of a statement. I kept

FINISHED QUILT SIZE: 35" x 35"   FINISHED BLOCK SIZE: 3½" x 3½"

sewing until I had 49 blocks to achieve the scrappy look I wanted. I think 36 blocks might have worked, except that I wanted to feature a Star block in the center, so I needed an uneven number of blocks in the rows.

This is one of those quilts where you will spend as much time selecting and cutting fabric as you will sewing and quilting. I recommend placing your setting fabric on your design wall and then adding the blocks to it as you

piece them. This way, you can see what your quilt will look like.

Be sure to pull out your stripes and other interesting fabric patterns for use in this quilt. Please don't match everything—using several shades of a color is much more interesting.

Enjoy your own fabric adventure!

Fabrics

Block piecing: Approximately 1½ yards assorted fabric in light, medium, and dark values for blocks (refer to the color photo for guidance in choosing fabrics)

Blue stripe: 1 yard for three borders

Blue print: 1 yard for sashing and fourth border

Soft red print: 1¼ yards for backing

Another red print: ¼ yard for single-thickness binding

Batting: 40" x 40"

Cutting

Album Cross Blocks

For *each* block, you will need 1 set (44 sets total):
From dark-value fabric:
❀ Cut 1 square 1⁹/₁₆" x 1⁹/₁₆" for the center square.

From medium-value fabric:
❀ Cut 1 strip 1⁹/₁₆" x 12½", then cut into 4 rectangles 1⁹/₁₆" x 3" for the legs of the cross.

From contrasting fabric:
❀ Cut 1 square 3³/₈" x 3³/₈", then cut into quarter-square triangles for the background. (Refer to pages 15–16 for instructions on cutting triangles.)

Four-Patch Blocks

For *each* block, you will need 1 set (make 4 blocks)
From a dark fabric:
❀ Cut 2 squares 1³/₄" x 1³/₄" for the Four-Patch block.

From a medium fabric:
❀ Cut 2 squares 1³/₄" x 1³/₄" for the Four-Patch block.

From a third fabric:
❀ Cut 2 squares 2⁵/₈" x 2⁵/₈", then cut half-square triangles for the background. (Refer to pages 15–16 for instructions.)

SEWING THE BLOCKS

Sew each block as you cut it out. Place the block on your design wall atop the setting fabric before making your fabric selections for the next block. By proceeding in this way, you will see which colors you need to add to your quilt, as well as whether the fabric designs are adding extra motion to the quilt. Examine the stripes. Try fussy cutting them in different directions and placements to find which adds the most interest to your quilt.

LeMoyne Star Block (for center)

From a brown fabric:
❀ Cut 1 strip 1½" x 12½" for 4 star sections.

From a red/rust fabric:
❀ Cut 1 strip 1½" x 12½" for 4 star sections.

Recut these 2 strips to form the **diamond segments**: Place your ruler's 45° line along the long (or bottom) edge of a strip near the end. Trim off the end triangle. Turn the mat 180° and slide the ruler to find the 1½" marking. Be sure that the 1½" marking is along the newly cut edge and the 45° line is on the bottom edge of the strip. Cut the diamond. Continue cutting the other 3 pieces from this strip.

(Cutting continued on next page.)

From the background fabric:

❀ Cut 4 squares 2" x 2" for the background corners.

❀ Cut 1 square 3¼" x 3¼", then cut into quarter-square triangles. (Refer to pages 15–16 for instructions.)

From a dark brown fabric:

❀ Cut 2 strips 1" x 5½" to frame the LeMoyne Star block.

❀ Cut 2 strips 1" x 6½" to frame the LeMoyne Star block.

Sashing and bottom border

From the blue print fabric:

❀ Cut 40 strips 1½" x 4" for horizontal sashing.

❀ Cut 4 strips 1½" x 13" for vertical sashing in the center area.

❀ Cut 4 strips 1½" x 31" for vertical sashing in the side areas.

❀ Cut 1 strip 2½" x 31" for the bottom border.

Top and side borders

From the blue stripe fabric:

❀ Cut 1 strip 2½" x 31" for the top border.

❀ Cut 2 strips 2½" x 35" for the side borders.

Binding

From the red print:

❀ Cut 4 strips 1⅛" x the width of the fabric for the single-thickness binding. (Refer to Single-Thickness Binding on pages 17–19.)

Make the Blocks

ALBUM CROSS BLOCKS

1. Arrange an Album Cross block set as shown.

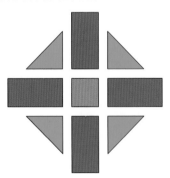

Arrange Album Cross block set.

2. Sew a triangle to one side of a rectangle, making sure to align the short, straight edge of the triangle with the inside edge of the rectangle. Sew a triangle in the same manner to the opposite side of the rectangle. Press toward the triangles. Repeat to make the second unit.

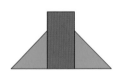

Sew triangles to sides of rectangle.

3. Sew the short ends of 2 rectangles to opposite sides of the center square. Press toward the center.

Sew rectangles to center square.

4. Sew a triangle unit to the center unit, matching the seam intersections. Sew the other triangle unit to the opposite side of center unit, matching the seam intersections. Use the Clipping Trick (refer to page 17) at the seam intersections. Press the seams toward the triangles, the center toward the center, and the clipped intersections open.

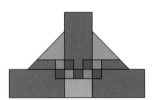

Use Clipping Trick and press seams as directed.

5. With a 4" square ruler, align the 45° lines along the center square and the 2" vertical line through the diagonal of the center square. Use your rotary cutter to trim the excess fabric on both sides of the ruler.

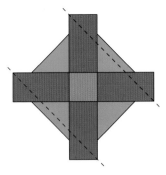

Trim excess fabric.

6. Rotate the ruler to trim the remaining 2 sides in the same manner. Your block will now measure 4" square and will finish 3½" square.

7. Repeat Steps 1 through 6 to make the remaining 43 Album Cross blocks.

Make 44 blocks.

LEMOYNE STAR BLOCK

1. On the wrong sides of the fabric pieces for this block, mark dots where the seamlines intersect. Use your ruler to draw lines a scant ¼" from the cut edge near the corners. Make sure the lines intersect or form an X.

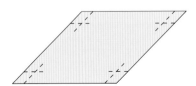

Mark all corners on diamond.

Mark all corners on square.

Mark all corners on triangle.

2. Lay out the pieces to form the Star block, alternating the colors of the diamond segments. Arrange the background triangles and corners to form the block.

3. Pin 2 diamonds together, matching the dots. Use a short stitch length to sew toward the center from dot to dot. Backstitch at each dot. You may need to pivot at the dot and sew back over the first few stitches to lock them. Do not sew across the seam allowances.

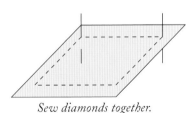

Sew diamonds together.

4. Repeat Steps 1 through 3 for the 3 remaining sets of diamonds. Note that the diamonds must have the same fabric sequence. Carefully press the seams toward the dark fabric.

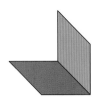

Sew remaining diamonds.

5. To inset the corner squares into the diamond unit, match the dots and pin a side in place. Sew from dot to dot and backstitch.

6. Pin the adjacent side in place, matching the dots. Sew and backstitch.

Match dots, pin, and sew.

7. Repeat Steps 5 and 6 for the 3 remaining sets of diamonds. Carefully press the seams toward the background fabric.

8. To join 2 quarters to form a half star, match the dots and pin one side. Sew toward the center from dot to dot and backstitch. Repeat for the other 2 quarters. Press this seam toward the lighter fabric (eventually, the seams will be circular, all going in the same direction).

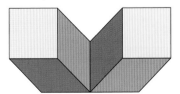

Join quarters.

9. To inset a background triangle, match the dots and pin one side. Sew and backstitch. Pin the other side, matching the dots. Sew and backstitch. Repeat for the other half star. Press the seams toward the background fabric.

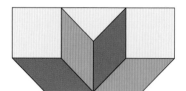

Insert background triangle.

10. To join the 2 half stars, match the dots and pin one side of a diamond. Sew and backstitch. Pin the other side of a diamond, matching the dots. Sew and backstitch. (*Do not sew across the center.*) Make sure the center closes up. Continue to press the seams in one direction (circular). Carefully straighten the center diamond points to form a swirl, making sure that the points make a small star. Press the center flat.

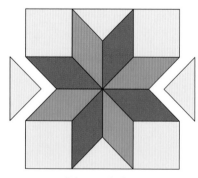

Join star halves.

11. Repeat Step 9 for the remaining triangles. Press the seams toward the background fabric.

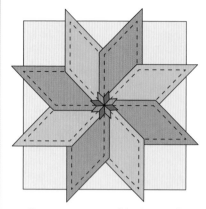

Press seams toward background.

12. Your LeMoyne Star block should square to 5½" x 5½" (finish 5" square).

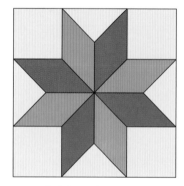

LeMoyne Star block

13. To frame the LeMoyne Star block, sew 2 of the dark brown 1" x 5½" strips to the sides of the block. Press toward the dark brown strips.

14. Take the 2 dark brown 1" x 6½" strips, center them on the LeMoyne Star block, and sew them to the top and bottom. Press toward the dark brown strips.

15. Use your rotary cutter and a 6" ruler to trim the dark fabric and square the block to 6" x 6". Place the 3" line down the center of the LeMoyne Star block to make sure that you trim evenly.

FOUR-PATCH BLOCKS

1. Arrange the squares to form the Four-Patch. Sew the top squares together. Sew the bottom squares together. Press toward the dark fabric.

2. Sew the units together, matching the seam intersection. Press the seam open.

3. Sew 2 of the half-square triangles to opposite sides of the Four-Patch. Press toward the triangles.

4. Sew the remaining 2 half-square triangles to opposite sides of the Four-Patch. Press toward the triangles.

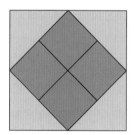

Sew half-square triangles to Four-Patch.

5. Square to measure 4" x 4".

6. Repeat Steps 1 through 5 to make 3 more Four-Patches in a square for the corners.

Assemble the Quilt Top

ALBUM CROSS BLOCKS

1. Arrange the Album Cross blocks, the LeMoyne Star block in the center, and the Four-Patch blocks in the corners to make 7 rows of 7 blocks.

2. Place the short sashing strips on the horizontal (the bottom of the blocks).

3. Place the long sashing strips on the vertical.

SEWING TIPS

Pair an Album Cross block with a sashing strip, right sides together. Using the walking foot on your sewing machine, sew with the block on the bottom. This will help prevent the bias-edged corners of the Album Cross blocks from stretching.

4. Sew the blocks and sashings to make vertical rows. Press the seams toward the sashing.

5. Sew 2 of the 1½" x 13" sashing strips to the top center vertical row of the Album Cross blocks. Press toward the sashing.

6. Sew 2 of the 1½" x 13" sashing strips to the bottom center vertical row of the Album Cross blocks. Press toward the sashing.

7. Sew these 2 sets of Album Cross blocks to the top and bottom of the center LeMoyne Star framed block.

8. Pin and sew a 1½" x 31" sashing strip, right sides together, to the right side of vertical row 1. Press toward the sashing.

9. Pin and sew vertical row 2, right sides together, to the sashing strip on vertical row 1. Press toward the sashing.

10. Pin and sew a 1½" x 31" sashing strip, right sides together, to the right side of vertical row 2. Press toward the sashing.

11. Pin and sew vertical row 3, right sides together, to the sashing strip on vertical row 2. Press toward the sashing.

12. Pin and sew vertical row 4 (center row), right sides together, matching the seam intersections, to the right side of vertical row 3. Press toward the sashing.

13. Continue sewing the quilt top in this manner.

BORDER

1. Pin and sew the blue print 2½" x 31" border to the bottom of the quilt top. Press toward the border.

2. Pin and sew 1 blue stripe 2½" x 31" border to the top of the quilt top. Press toward the border.

3. Pin and sew 2 blue stripe 2½" x 35" borders to the sides of the quilt top. Press toward the border.

Finish the Quilt

1. Layer the backing, batting, and quilt top. Baste.

2. Quilt as desired, or follow the Suggested Quilting Design (page 28).

3. Bind. (Refer to Single-Thickness Binding on pages 17–19.)

BASTING TIPS

Consider taking your quilt layers to a longarm machine quilter to have your quilt basted for a small fee. I have a friend who machine bastes in horizontal rows 2" apart. This method works nicely for hand quilting because there are no pins to catch the thread and you can save time, as well as your back and knees, compared with thread basting by hand.

SUGGESTED QUILTING DESIGN

Refer to page 14 for thread suggestions.

1. Quilt the LeMoyne Star block seams in-the-ditch.

2. Quilt the outside edge of the LeMoyne Star block in-the-ditch.

3. Carefully quilt the narrow dark brown frame in-the-ditch.

4. Quilt the 44 Album Cross block seams in-the-ditch.

5. Quilt in-the-ditch all the quilt block edges next to the sashings from border edge to border edge.

Cross continuous quilting lines over the sashing intersections to form a square on each intersection.

6. Quilt down the center of each sashing strip in a continuous line from border edge to border edge.

7. Quilt in-the-ditch next to the border edge.

8. Quilt the Four-Patch blocks in-the-ditch next to the triangles. Quilt an X across the Four-Patch.

9. Quilt the border by continuing the diagonal lines established by the Album Cross blocks across to the outer edge of the border.

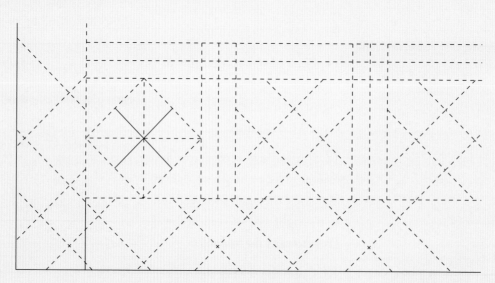

Block, sashing, and border quilting

Rebecca's Baskets II

FINISHED QUILT SIZE: 36" x 36"   FINISHED BLOCK SIZE: 5¼" x 5¼"

I saw this wonderful double-handled basket block in an antique indigo crib quilt. I had never seen a basket block with both a pieced triangle handle and an appliqué handle in the same block. The antique quilt was set square, and all the basket blocks headed in the same direction. It had sashings in the center but no border or outer sashing.

I decided to make a pink and brown version (I am making my own collection of pink and brown quilts). One change seemed obvious: make only the basket brown and both the appliqué and pieced handles double-pink. The

next step was multiple backgrounds, but using only one background per block.

I began by making the blocks. As I tried different arrangements of the blocks, I came up with this setting, which resulted in the secondary pattern that appears when the pieced handles come together to form Flying Geese—interesting, don't you think? Of course this element had to be repeated and became the inner Double Sawtooth border to set off the center.

I fell in love with the block and have used it in several projects, hence the "II" in the title of this quilt.

Fabrics

❋ **Assorted browns:** 16 pieces no smaller than $6\frac{1}{2}"$ x $6\frac{1}{2}"$ square for the baskets

❋ **Assorted pinks:** 10 pieces no smaller than $12\frac{1}{2}"$ x $12\frac{1}{2}"$ square for the basket handles and Double Sawtooth border piecing

❋ **Assorted beige/light tan prints:** 16 fat quarters for background of the basket blocks and Double Sawtooth border piecing

❋ **Dark purple/brown print:** $\frac{5}{8}$ yard for sashing, cornerstones, and binding

❋ **Medium brown larger scale print:** 1 yard for outer border

❋ **Interesting print:** $1\frac{1}{4}$ yards for backing

❋ **Batting:** 42" x 42"

Cutting

Basket Blocks

From each of the 16 **brown fabrics:**

❋ Cut 1 square $2\frac{1}{8}"$ x $2\frac{1}{8}"$, then cut half-square triangles for the basket feet (G). (Refer to pages 15–16 for instructions on cutting triangles.)

❋ Cut 1 square $3\frac{7}{8}"$ x $3\frac{7}{8}"$, then cut a half-square triangle for the basket (D). (Refer to pages 15–16 for instructions.) You will need only 1 triangle per block.

From the 10 **pink fabrics:**

❋ Make 16 sets: cut 3 squares 2" x 2" for the half-square triangles (A) and 1 rectangle $2\frac{1}{2}"$ x 4" for the appliqué handle.

From each of the 16 **background fabrics:**

❋ Cut 1 square $3\frac{7}{8}"$ x $3\frac{7}{8}"$, then cut half-square triangles (C). One triangle is for the appliqué handle background, and the other goes below the basket feet. This base triangle will be trimmed later.

❋ Cut 3 squares 2" x 2" for the half-square triangles (B).

❋ Cut 1 square $1\frac{1}{2}"$ x $1\frac{1}{2}"$ for the basket background (E).

❋ Cut 2 rectangles $1\frac{3}{4}"$ x $3\frac{1}{4}"$ for basket side background (F).

Sashing

From the **dark purple/brown print fabric:**

❋ Cut 12 strips $1\frac{1}{2}"$ x 11" for sashing.

From a **pink fabric:**

❋ Cut 9 squares $1\frac{1}{2}"$ x $1\frac{1}{2}"$ for the cornerstones.

Double Sawtooth Border

From the 10 assorted **pink fabrics:**

❋ Cut 48 squares 4" x 4" for the Double Sawtooth border.

From the 16 assorted **background fabrics:**

❋ Cut 48 squares 4" x 4" for the Double Sawtooth border.

From the **dark purple/brown print fabric:**

❋ Cut 4 squares $2\frac{1}{2}"$ x $2\frac{1}{2}"$ for the cornerstones.

Outer Border

From the **medium brown fabric:**

❋ Cut 4 strips $4\frac{1}{2}"$ x $28\frac{1}{2}"$ for the border.

From the **dark purple/brown print fabric:**

❋ Cut 4 squares $4\frac{1}{2}"$ x $4\frac{1}{2}"$ for the cornerstones.

Binding

From the **dark purple/brown print fabric:**

❋ Cut 4 strips $1\frac{1}{8}"$ x the width of the fabric for single-thickness binding. (Refer to Single-Thickness Binding on pages 17–19.)

Make the Blocks

HALF-SQUARE TRIANGLE UNITS

1. Make half-square triangle units for the basket points: pair up the 3 sets of 2" squares of pink and background fabrics, right sides together.

Pair up fabrics.

2. Draw a diagonal line on the light squares and sew 1/4" on each side of the diagonal line.

Sew 1/4" on each side of line.

3. Cut apart on the diagonal line and press toward the pink fabric. Square up to 1½" x 1½".

Make 6.

BASKET HANDLES

1. Use template plastic (or your favorite method) to make a template for the basket handle. Place the template plastic over the drawing (on page 33), trace, and cut out on the drawn line.

2. Place the template on the right side of a pink fabric. Draw around the template. Cut out the shape, leaving a fat 1/8" turn-under allowance.

3. Position the handle on a background triangle (C) so the outside finished edge of the handle is about 1/2" from the raw edge of the background triangle. Refer to the quilt photo to be sure you have the correct placement. Stitch the inside curve of the handle first. (Refer to Needle-turn Appliqué on pages 19–21.)

ASSEMBLE THE BLOCKS

1. Pin and sew the light triangle with the appliqué handle to a large brown triangle (D). Press toward the dark triangle. The resulting square should measure 3½" x 3½".

2. Sew together 3 half-square triangle units to make 2 rows of basket points. Press toward the dark fabric. Add a 1½" background square (E) to the end of one of the rows. Press this last seam toward the corner, but be sure to note the direction of the triangles.

3. Sew the basket point rows to the center square (C/D). Press toward the center. Use the Clipping Trick (refer to page 17) at the seam intersection at the top square of the basket block. This allows you to press the basket point rows toward the center and the top seams toward the top square. Press the clipped intersection open.

4. Sew the basket feet triangles (G) to the side rectangles (F). Press toward the triangle.

5. Sew the side units (F/G) to the block. Press toward the side units.

6. The large background triangle (C) is oversized, so you need to center it. Sew, and then press the seam allowances toward the background triangle.

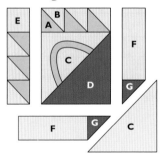

Basket Block Assembly
Make 16.

7. Trim the bottom triangle by squaring the block to 5¾" x 5¾".

8. Make 16 basket blocks.

Assemble the Quilt Top

BASKET BLOCKS

1. Arrange the basket blocks to make 4 sets of four-block units, with the basket tops meeting in the center. Notice the Flying Geese secondary pattern that forms where the blocks meet.

A secondary pattern forms where the blocks meet.

2. Pin and sew the top 2 blocks, matching the seam intersections. Press the seam open. Repeat for the bottom 2 blocks.

3. Pin and sew the top unit to the bottom unit, matching the seam intersections. Press the seam open.

4. Sew the other blocks into four-block units in the same manner.

5. Arrange the block units with the sashing and cornerstones.

6. Sew the blocks and vertical sashings into rows. Press the seams toward the sashings.

7. Join the horizontal sashing and cornerstones into rows. Press the seams toward the sashings.

8. Pin and sew the sashing rows and block unit rows, matching the seam intersections. Use the Clipping Trick (refer to page 17) at the seam intersections. Press the blocks toward the sashing, the cornerstones toward the sashing, and the seam intersections open.

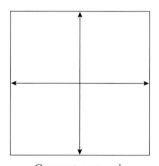

Cornerstone pressing

Center Section Assembly

DOUBLE SAWTOOTH BORDER

This border is designed to echo the Flying Geese units that appear when the 4 pieced basket blocks are joined.

1. Draw intersecting diagonal lines on the wrong sides of the 4" background squares. Layer the background and pink squares into 48 sets, right sides together. Stitch 1/4" on each side of the 2 drawn lines.

Stitch on both sides of the lines.

2. First cut horizontally and vertically through the center of the block.

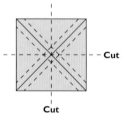

Cut horizontally and vertically.

3. Cut apart the squares on the drawn diagonal lines. Press toward the pink fabric. Square to measure 1 1/2" x 1 1/2" to get the 192 triangle squares needed for the Double Sawtooth border.

4. Arrange the triangle squares as shown, noting the direction of the triangles.

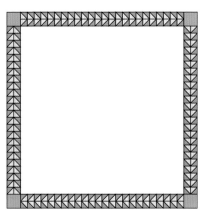

Note the direction of the triangles.

5. Sew together pairs of the triangle squares to form Flying Geese units. Press the seams open. Make 96 Flying Geese units.

6. Sew together 24 Flying Geese units for each border. Press the seams toward the pink fabric.

7. Sew the border units to the top and bottom of the quilt, and press toward the center of the quilt top.

8. Sew the cornerstones to the ends of the 2 remaining borders. Press toward the cornerstones. Pin, matching the seam intersections, and sew. Press toward the center.

9. The quilt top should measure 28½" x 28½".

OUTER BORDER

1. Pin and sew 2 of the outer border strips to the top and bottom of the quilt. Press toward the border.

2. Sew the cornerstones to the ends of the 2 remaining borders.

Press toward the border. Pin the borders to the sides of the quilt, matching the seam intersections, and sew. Press toward the border.

Finish the Quilt

1. Layer the backing, batting, and quilt top. Baste.

2. Quilt as desired, or follow the Suggested Quilting Design.

3. Bind. (Refer to Single-Thickness Binding on pages 17–19.)

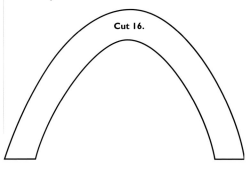

Cut 16.

Trace to make a template for the basket handle.

SUGGESTED QUILTING DESIGN

Refer to page 14 for thread suggestions.

1. Quilt the basket blocks in-the-ditch along the sashing.

2. Quilt the basket seams in-the-ditch.

3. Quilt 2 parallel lines in the rectangles.

4. Quilt a triangle in the triangle at the bottom of the basket.

5. Quilt the brown basket triangle in 2 chevron lines parallel to the edge of the basket, about ½" apart.

6. Quilt the appliqué handle in-the-ditch on both

sides and echo a smaller curve on the inner side about ¼" away.

7. Quilt down the middle of all the sashing strips.

8. Quilt the Double Sawtooth border to look like a Flying Geese unit (the larger triangle). Quilt in-the-ditch along each long side.

9. Quilt the outer border in diagonal lines about ⅝" apart. Use the Flying Geese units to establish the line spacing.

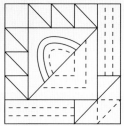

Basket block quilting

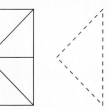

Double Sawtooth border quilting

Forever Stars

FINISHED QUILT SIZE: 37½" x 37½"   FINISHED BLOCK SIZE: 5½" x 5½"

This quilt is adapted from an antique bed-sized quilt that features red stars on a solid mustard background with an alternate muslin block. It was a great graphic quilt to re-create on a smaller scale.

To re-create a vintage look, use four or five different red solid fabrics in slightly different shades to give the appearance of fabrics that have faded at different rates. Because I like the texture provided by prints, I appliquéd the stars to a tan mini-check. Then my five-year plan kicked in. It took me five years to find the right alternate block fabric. Annually, I auditioned the Star blocks on various prints—blues, greens, browns, reds—but nothing spoke to me. I just couldn't bring myself to use muslin; I don't do muslin. I put the Star blocks away several times in frustration, and then finally, five years later, I found and auditioned the wonderful mustard print. It spoke to me, and I could complete the quilt!

This quilt has been a perfect addition to our home.

Fabrics

Red solids: Fat quarters of 4 or 5 different red solids for the stars, inner pieced border, and corner blocks

Tan mini-check: 1/2 yard for background and inner pieced border

Mustard print: 1 yard for border and alternate . blocks

Red ombre stripe: 1/4 yard for single-thickness binding

Homespun stripe: 1 1/4 yards for backing

Batting: 42" x 42"

Cutting

Stars

Make the star template (using the template pattern on page 37) from template plastic or use your favorite appliqué method. Trace around the template to create the turning line for your needle-turn appliqué.

From the various red fabrics:

❋ Cut 13 stars, adding a fat 1/8" turn-under allowance for the needle-turn hand appliqué. In my quilt, all the stars stand on 2 feet; but this is your quilt, and you can stand your stars however you wish.

From the tan mini-check fabric:

❋ Cut 13 squares 6" x 6" for star backgrounds.

From the mustard print fabric:

❋ Cut 12 squares 6" x 6" for alternate blocks.

Inner Pieced Border

From the tan mini-check fabric:

❋ Cut 60 squares 1 7/8" x 1 7/8" for the inner border.

From the red fabrics:

❋ Cut 28 squares 3 1/4" x 3 1/4" from the assorted red fabrics, then cut quarter-square triangles for inner border triangles. (Refer to pages 15–16 for triangle cutting instructions.)

❋ Cut 8 squares 2" x 2", then cut half-square triangles for the corners at the ends of the border rows. (Refer to pages 15–16 for instructions.)

Outer Border

From a red fabric:

❋ Cut 4 squares 3 1/2" x 3 1/2" for cornerstones.

From the mustard print fabric:

❋ Cut 4 strips lengthwise 3 1/2" x 31 1/2" for outer border.

Binding

From the red ombre stripe fabric:

❋ Cut 4 strips 1 1/8" x the width of the fabric for single-thickness binding. (Refer to Single-Thickness Binding on pages 17–19.)

Make the Blocks

APPLIQUÉ STAR BLOCKS

1. Appliqué the 13 stars to the background blocks. (Refer to Needle-turn Appliqué on pages 19–21 or use your favorite appliqué method.)

Assemble the Quilt Top

APPLIQUÉ STAR AND ALTERNATE BLOCKS

1. Sew the appliqué blocks and the alternate blocks in 5 rows of 5 blocks. Note the star block placement in the picture, as well as the direction of the star feet.

2. Pin the first row to the second row, matching the seam intersections. Sew.

3. Use the Clipping Trick at all the seam intersections (refer to page 17). Press all the seams toward the alternate blocks (mustard print).

4. Continue to sew the rows together.

5. Your quilt top should measure 28" x 28". This is important for the pieced border to fit properly.

INNER BORDER

1. Sew the short sides of 2 quarter-square red triangles to opposite sides of a tan square. Press the seams toward the red triangles.

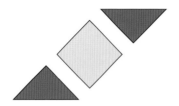

Sew triangles to squares.

2. Your units should look like this. Make 60 units.

Make 60.

3. Sew these units together to form 2 rows of 14 squares, matching the seam intersections. Do not sew quarter-square triangles to the 4 end squares.

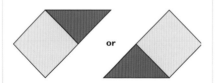

Sew end units.

4. Sew the remaining units together to form 2 rows of 16 squares, matching the seam intersections. Do not sew quarter-square triangles to the 4 end squares.

5. Use the Clipping Trick at all the seam intersections. Press all the seams toward the red triangles.

6. Sew the long sides of 2 half-square red triangles to the ends of

Half-square triangles square off the pieced border rows.

7. Pin the 2 shorter pieced borders to opposite sides of the quilt top. Sew. Press toward the center.

8. Pin the 2 remaining pieced borders to the quilt top. Sew. Press toward the center.

9. Your quilt top should measure 31½" x 31½".

OUTER BORDER

1. Pin 2 of the mustard border strips to opposite sides of the quilt. Sew. Press toward the border.

2. Sew the red corner blocks to the ends of the 2 remaining border strips. Press toward the border.

3. Pin these borders to the quilt, matching the seam intersections. Sew. Press toward the border. Use the Clipping Trick for the intersecting corners.

4. Your top should measure 37½" x 37½".

Finish the Quilt

1. Layer the backing, batting, and quilt top. Baste.

2. Quilt as desired, or follow the Suggested Quilting Design.

3. Bind. (Refer to Single-Thickness Binding on pages 17–19.)

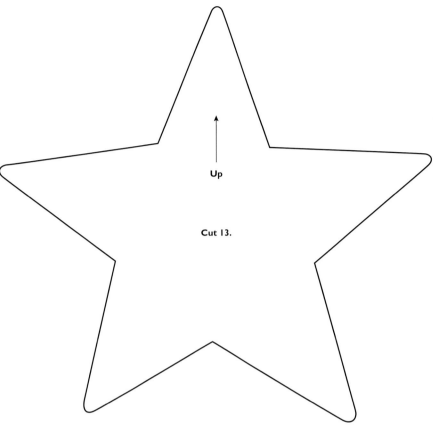

Up

Cut 13.

Star template

SUGGESTED QUILTING DESIGN

Refer to page 14 for thread suggestions.

1. Quilt the blocks in-the-ditch along the block seams, both vertically and horizontally.

2. Quilt in-the-ditch on each side of the pieced inner border.

3. Quilt in-the-ditch next to the star appliqué. Echo the quilt lines approximately ⅜" apart around the stars.

4. Crosshatch the alternate blocks with the lines ¾" apart. The grid is centered over the corner, not from corner to corner.

Alternate block quilting

5. Quilt in-the-ditch inside each square of the pieced inner border. You can make a continuous zigzag quilting line.

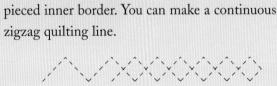

Inner border quilting

6. Use a ruler and a chalk wheel fabric marker to extend the inner border diagonal lines into the outer border and over the corner blocks. You will have a larger crosshatch quilting pattern in the outer border.

Concentric Log Cabin

This unique version of the timeless Log Cabin block was inspired by my friend's turn-of-the-century, bed-sized quilt top. The quilt top consisted of one very large Log Cabin block extending from side to side. To elongate it, the quilt-maker added extra logs across the top and bottom, changed it from a square to rectangle, and sized it to fit a bed. You will be amazed to know that the logs in the antique quilt are 1/2" wide (finished). Even more amazing, the top, made of turn-of-the-century shirtings and black and burgundy prints, is entirely hand pieced!

After seeing the quilt top, I decided to preserve my memory of a nice day spent with a quilting friend discussing antique quilts. My quilt is only 29" square, in various shades and hues of reds and browns (a favorite color combination of mine). Every time I look at it, I think of the pleasant day spent with my friend.

This timeless variation on the Log Cabin block has a wonderful graphic appeal. With careful fabric choices, you can easily bring it into the twenty-first century.

FINISHED QUILT SIZE: 29½" x 29½"

PIECING

Consistent, accurate piecing and careful pressing are important to make this project successful.

Fabrics

Assorted fabrics: Various pieces ¼ to ⅞ yard for the Log Cabin logs

Red print: 1 piece no smaller than 3" x 3" for the center square

Dark red print: 1 yard for the last row or border

Eggplant stripe fabric: ¼ yard for single-thickness binding (or ½ yard if you wish to cut a stripe fabric on the diagonal for an accent)

Brown, red, and tan print: 1 yard for backing

Batting: 35" x 35"

Cutting

Log Cabin

From the red print fabric:
❀ Cut 1 square 2½" x 2½" for the center.

From the Log Cabin logs fabrics:
❀ Cut 1" x the length of the chosen fabric. You may need to cut more strips as the quilt grows.
❀ Cut 25 rounds 1" wide for the logs. One round consists of all four sides.

From the dark red print fabric used for the last row:
❀ Cut 2 strips 1¼" x 29".
❀ Cut 2 strips 1¼" x 27½".

Binding

From the eggplant stripe fabric:
❀ Cut 4 strips 1⅛" x the width of the fabric for the single-thickness binding. (Refer to Single-Thickness Binding on pages 17–19.) If you are fortunate enough to find an eggplant stripe fabric, cut it at an approximately 30° angle to elongate the stripe effect in the binding.

Make the Quilt

1. Assemble the quilt top following the Courthouse Steps sequence (see page 54). Sew strips on opposite sides of the block, and then trim them to the correct length.

2. Repeat for the other 2 strips to complete each round of logs with the same fabric color or hue.

(see page 54)

FOR A FLAT QUILT TOP

1. On the first round (all 4 sides), sew with the center block unit right side up and the 1" strip placed on top of the unit, right sides together.

2. On the second round (all 4 sides), sew with the center block unit wrong side up and placed on the 1" strip, right sides together..

3. Alternate this sewing sequence (center unit right side up, then wrong side up) when assembling your quilt top. If strips are added with the center unit consistently in the same position, some sewing machines will pull the fabric, causing the quilt to cup so it will not lie flat. Ask me how I know!

4. Be very careful when pressing the strips, because you do not want the top to bow out. Press in an up-and-down motion; do not iron.

3. For the first round, sew the 1" strip to opposite sides of the red print square. Carefully press toward the strips. Use your rotary cutter and ruler to trim the unit to 2½" x 3½".

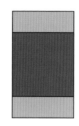

Sew first strip, then trim.

4. Sew the same 1" strip to opposite sides of the red print center square. Carefully press toward the strips. Use your rotary cutter and ruler to trim the unit to 3½" x 3½".

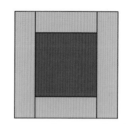

Sew same strip to opposite sides.

5. For the second round, sew the selected 1" strip to opposite sides of the unit. Press toward the strips. Use your rotary cutter and ruler to trim the unit to 3½" x 4½".

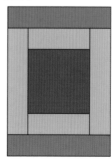

Sew next strip to opposite sides.

6. Sew the same 1" strip to opposite sides of the unit. Press toward the strip. Use your rotary cutter and ruler to trim the unit to 4½" x 4½".

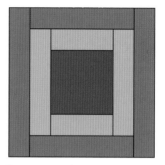

Sew same strip to opposite sides.

7. Continue sewing the next 23 rounds in the same manner. With each round, your trimming measurements expand in 1" increments.

8. Add the last row with the dark red print strips in the same manner. These strips are a bit wider to create the illusion of a narrow border.

Finish the Quilt

1. Layer the backing, batting, and quilt top. Baste.

2. Quilt as desired, or follow the Suggested Quilting Design.

3. Bind. (Refer to Single-Thickness Binding on pages 17–19.)

Photo by Mark Jewell

SUGGESTED QUILTING DESIGN

Refer to page 14 for thread suggestions.

1. Quilt each block in concentric squares, approximately ⅛" from the ditch so the stitches are visible. With practice, you can eyeball all these quilting lines.

2. Bind the quilt, then go back and quilt ⅛" from the binding on the last row

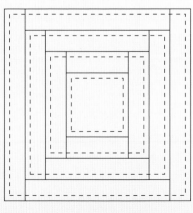

Log Cabin quilting

Mary's Stars

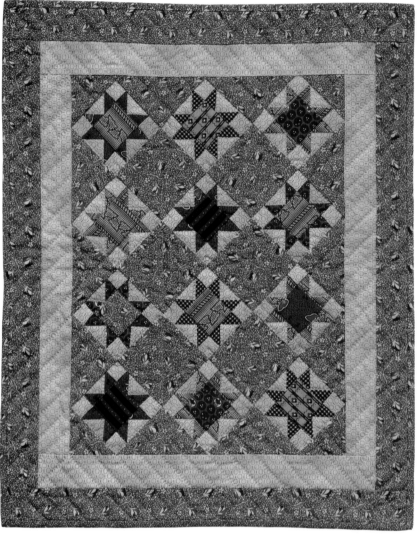

FINISHED QUILT SIZE: 16¼" x 20"   FINISHED BLOCK SIZE: 2½" x 2½"

This darling doll quilt was inspired by a circa 1860 doll quilt owned by Mary Ghormley of Lincoln, Nebraska. Assembling these charming small stars is a breeze when using modern techniques and sewing machines. Whereas Mary's antique doll quilt was made with scrappy brown stars and pink setting, I made my version in browns, using fabrics from the first three lines that I designed for Andover Fabrics.

Eleven of the star blocks are made with three fabrics and one is made with two fabrics. You will have fun pairing up the six fabrics to make scrappy star blocks. Refer to the color picture of the quilt for help.

Remember: accurate piecing skills will make sewing these small blocks a breeze.

Fabrics

Medium brown print: 5/8 yard for single-thickness binding, setting, and outer border

Light tan: fat quarter for inner border and Star block backgrounds

Assorted browns: 6 pieces no smaller than 9" x 10" for Star block piecing (Refer to the color picture for guidance in choosing fabric.)

Medium brown print: 3/4 yard for backing

Batting: 20" x 24"

Cutting

Star Blocks

From the **6 brown fabrics:**
❋ Cut 12 squares 1 3/4" x 1 3/4" for the centers of the Star blocks.

❋ Cut 48 squares 1 1/2" x 1 1/2" (in sets of 4) for the star points.

From the **light tan fabric:**
❋ Cut 12 squares 2 1/2" x 2 1/2" for the large triangles between star points.

❋ Cut 48 squares 1 1/8" x 1 1/8" for the corners in the Star blocks.

Setting

From the **medium brown print fabric:**
❋ Cut 6 squares 3" x 3" for alternate blocks.

❋ Cut 3 squares 5 3/4" x 5 3/4", then cut each into quarter-square triangles for the setting triangles.

❋ Cut 2 squares 3 1/2" x 3 1/2", then cut half-square triangles for the corners.

(The setting and corner triangles are slightly over-sized and will be trimmed after sewing. Refer to pages 15–16 for instructions on cutting triangles.)

Inner Border

From the **light tan fabric:**
❋ Cut 2 strips lengthwise 1 3/4" x 15" for the sides of the inner border.

❋ Cut 2 strips lengthwise 1 3/4" x 13 3/4" for the top and bottom of the inner border.

Outer Border

From the **medium brown print fabric:**
❋ Cut 2 strips lengthwise 1 3/4" x 17 1/2" for the sides of the outer border.

❋ Cut 2 strips lengthwise 1 3/4" x 16 1/4" for the top and bottom of the outer border.

Binding

From the **medium brown print fabric:**
❋ Cut 2 strips 1 1/8" x the width of the fabric for single-thickness binding. (Refer to Single-Thickness Binding on pages 17–19.)

Make the Blocks

SAWTOOTH STAR BLOCKS

To make the Sawtooth Star blocks scrappy, I used 2 fabrics in 1 block and 3 fabrics in the remaining 11 blocks. See the photograph for guidance in arranging the assorted fabrics.

Flying Geese Unit

This method uses 5 squares to make 4 Flying Geese units, which makes sewing the Sawtooth Star blocks easy.

If you use this piecing technique with an accurate, scant 1/4" seam allowance, the Flying Geese will come out just the right size, with no fabric waste. Each set of squares makes 4 identical Flying Geese units.

1. For each set of 4 Flying Geese units, select 1 of the light tan 2 1/2" squares and 4 identical brown 1 1/2" squares.

2. Draw a diagonal line on the wrong side of each of the 1 1/2" brown squares.

3. Place two of the 1 1/2" brown squares on opposite corners of the 2 1/2" light tan fabric square, right sides together and aligned with the outer edges. Note how the brown squares overlap in the center.

4. Sew a scant 1/4" seam on each side of the drawn lines.

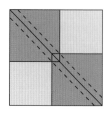

Note the overlap in the center; the dashed lines are the stitching lines.

5. Cut apart on the drawn line.

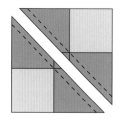

Cut apart.

6. Press toward the small triangles.

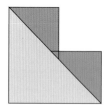

Press toward small triangles.

7. Place a 1 1/2" brown square on the corner of the large triangle. Note that the diagonal line points toward the center. Sew a scant 1/4" seam on each side of the drawn line. Repeat with the other unit.

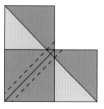

Sew.

8. Cut apart on the drawn line, and press toward the small triangles. You will have 4 identical Flying Geese units. Use your rotary cutter and a ruler with a 1/8" grid to **carefully cut the units to 1 1/8" x 1 3/4".**

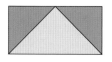

Trim.

Assemble the Blocks

1. Arrange the 4 Flying Geese segments, a 1 3/4" brown center square, and 4 of the 1 1/8" background corners, as shown.

2. Sew a background corner to each side of 2 Flying Geese segments. Sew 2 Flying Geese segments to each side of the brown center square. Press; the arrows indicate pressing directions.

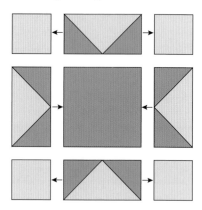

Sew Flying Geese to center square.

3. Pin row 1 to row 2, matching the seam intersections. Sew. Pin row 3 to row 2, matching the seam intersections. Sew.

4. Use the Clipping Trick (refer to page 17). Press the center area of the seam toward the center, press the outer seam toward the corners, and press the seam intersections open. Repeat for the other seam.

5. Square the block to 3" x 3".

6. Sew the remaining 11 blocks.

Assemble the Quilt Top

STAR AND ALTERNATE BLOCKS

1. Arrange the 12 Star blocks to make 4 rows of 3 blocks on point. Fill in with the 6 alternate block squares. Arrange the setting triangles and corners. Sew the blocks in diagonal rows. Press the seams toward the setting blocks or triangles.

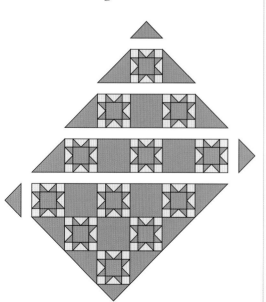

Sew in diagonal rows.

2. Pin the first row to the second row, matching the seam intersections. Sew the seam and use the Clipping Trick at the seam intersections. Press the seam intersections open, and press the remainder of the seam toward the setting blocks or triangles.

3. After you have sewn all the rows, add the corner triangles. Press toward the corners.

4. Carefully trim the excess on all 4 sides, leaving the ¼" seam allowance. Your quilt top should measure 11¼" x 15".

INNER BORDER

1. Pin and sew the 2 longer inner border strips to the sides of the quilt. Press toward the border.

2. Pin and sew the 2 remaining inner border strips to the top and bottom of the quilt. Press toward the border.

OUTER BORDER

1. Pin and sew the 2 longer outer border strips to the sides of the quilt. Press toward the outer border.

2. Pin and sew the 2 remaining outer border strips to the top and bottom of the quilt. Press toward the outer border. Your quilt top should measure 16¼" x 20".

USING A CAMERA

A camera is a wonderful quilt-making tool. If you use your camera, you will find that you love your completed project, and you won't suffer from the "what ifs."

❀ *Before sewing your quilt top, take pictures of different layouts to decide which version looks best.*

❀ *Use your camera to audition fabric choices for settings and borders.*

❀ *Digital cameras are even better because you don't have to wait for pictures to be developed. Digital cameras offer instant gratification when making your choices.*

Finish the Quilt

1. Layer the backing, batting, and quilt top. Baste.

2. Quilt as desired, or follow the Suggested Quilting Design (page 46).

3. Bind. (Refer to Single-Thickness Binding on pages 17–19.)

Resizing Flying Geese

1. A Flying Geese unit base is twice its height (for example, 1" x 2").

2. Use the half-square triangle rule: add $7/8$" to the finished height of your desired Flying Geese unit.

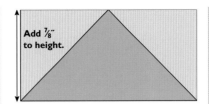

Square is height of finished unit plus $7/8$".

3. Make 4 squares of that measurement ($1 7/8$").

4. Use the quarter-square triangle rule: add $1 1/4$" to the finished base of your desired Flying Geese unit.

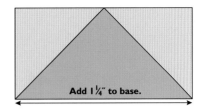

Square is width of finished base plus $1 1/4$".

5. Make 1 square of that measurement ($3 1/4$").

Any time you resize a Flying Geese unit, make a practice set to ensure its accuracy.

SUGGESTED QUILTING DESIGN

Refer to page 14 for thread suggestions.

1. Quilt the Star blocks in-the-ditch along the diagonal seams.

2. Quilt the Star block seams in-the-ditch. See the illustration for continuous-line quilting suggestions.

Star quilting

3. Quilt the alternate blocks in horizontal lines $1/2$" apart.

4. Consider the setting triangles and 2 borders as 1 unit for quilting. Quilt diagonal lines $5/8$" apart, using the Star block grid to establish the line.

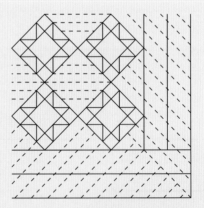

Border and setting triangles quilting

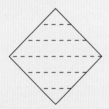

Alternate block quilting

Log Cabin
with Dogtooth Border

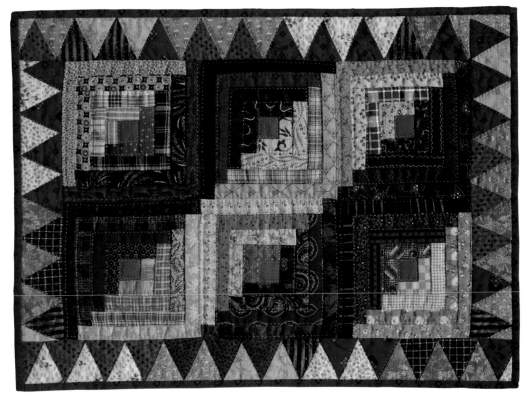

FINISHED QUILT SIZE: 17½" x 12¾"   FINISHED BLOCK SIZE: 4¾" x 4¾"

This charming small Log Cabin quilt is one of dozens I have made in different configurations, colors, border treatments, and sizes. For several years, I considered myself a Log Cabin queen during my quest to find different variations. I keep finding more variations of Log Cabins in my study of nineteenth-century quilts, and I hope to make versions of them someday.

On this quilt, I played with the Dogtooth border, whose unmatched appearance is perfect for this charming quilt. Although you would not want to use this border on a beautiful appliqué quilt, it adds a bit of whimsy on this small quilt.

In my quilts, my light fabrics are probably the same as your medium fabrics. I like the lower contrast in value in my quilts and think it contributes to an aged appearance.

There are 6 Log Cabin blocks in this quilt, each comprising 8 carefully selected fabrics, for a total of 48 different fabrics. The border alone has 8 assorted red prints and 6 assorted tan prints, for a total of 14 fabrics. Add this to the fabrics used in the piecing, and you have 62 different fabrics, plus the solid red used for the Log Cabin center and the brown print for the backing. The new total? 64 fabrics!

Fabrics

Assorted fabrics: 48 strips 1" x 12" from each fabric for the Log Cabin blocks

Note: Look for dark, rich colors with interesting patterns or prints in various scales, such as stripes and plaids in brick red, burgundy red, eggplant, brown, black, sage green, olive green, pumpkin, and dirty mustard. For your lights/mediums, find many shades of tan or taupe. Look at the photograph of the quilt for color guidance. I made this quilt in 1998, so the fabrics are older than that; some may even date back to the late 1980s.

Assorted red print fabrics: 8 pieces no smaller than 3" x 18" for the pieced border

Assorted tan print fabrics: 6 pieces no smaller than 3" x 18" for the pieced border

Red solid: 1 piece no smaller than 2" x 8" for the Log Cabin centers

Dark brick red print: fat quarter for single-thickness binding

Brown print: 1/2 yard for backing

Batting: 17" x 23"

Cutting

Log Cabin blocks

From the 48 assorted medium and dark fabrics:

❈ Cut 1" x 12" strips lengthwise (if you are cutting to take advantage of a stripe, cut crosswise for interest). Try fussy cutting some fabrics to add interest (perhaps to feature a motif or half a motif). By cutting the strips on the lengthwise grain, your blocks will have less give and will lie nice and flat. Strips cut crosswise have give to them and can stretch, which may be compounded by numerous crosswise-cut strips sewn together. This can create a wavy block.

From the red solid fabric:
❈ Cut 6 squares 1 1/4" x 1 1/4".

Borders

Make the template (using the template pattern on page 51) from template plastic and mark the arrow on the template for the "up" position. The direction of the arrow is very important because all sides of the triangle are not equal. The template includes the 1/4" seam allowance.

From the red fabric:
❈ Use the template on page 51 to cut 42 triangles.

From the tan fabric:
❈ Use the template to cut 42 triangles.

Binding

From the dark brick red print fabric:
❈ Cut 4 strips 1 1/8" x 22" from the fat quarter (cut crosswise to take advantage of the slight give) for single-thickness binding. (Refer to Single-Thickness Binding on pages 17–19.)

Make the Blocks

LOG CABIN BLOCKS

Piece your block in the following sequence:

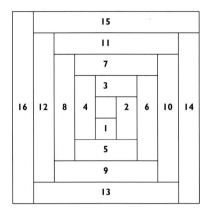

Piecing sequence

Note that each block uses 8 fabrics for the logs, 4 mediums and 4 darks. Each fabric is used 2 times in sequence.

1. The first medium fabric is #1, used in positions #1 and #2. Sew medium fabric #1 to the red center square, right sides together. Press toward the strip. Trim both ends with your rotary cutter and ruler to make a rectangle that measures 1 1/4" x 1 3/4".

First log sewn

2. Sew medium fabric #1 to the long side of the unit, right sides together. Press toward the strip. Trim both ends with your rotary cutter and ruler to make a square that measures 1 3/4" x 1 3/4".

Second log sewn

3. Use dark fabric #2 in positions #3 and #4. Sew dark fabric #2 to the red center square, right sides together. Press toward the strip. Trim both ends with your rotary cutter and ruler to make a rectangle that measures 2 1/4" x 1 3/4". Sew the same fabric to the adjacent side of the red square. Press toward the strip. Trim ends to square at 2 1/4".

First round of Log Cabin

4. Sew medium fabric #3 in position #5, right sides together. Press toward the strip and trim the ends, resulting in a rectangle. Sew medium fabric #3 in position #6, right sides together. Press toward the strip and trim the ends to make a square that measures 2 3/4" x 2 3/4".

Fabric #3 added

5. Sew dark fabric #4 in position #7, right sides together. Press toward the strip and trim the ends, resulting in a rectangle. Sew dark fabric #4 in position #8, right sides together. Press toward the strip and trim the ends to make a square that measures 3 1/4" x 3 1/4".

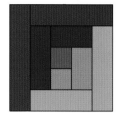

Second round of Log Cabin

6. Sew medium fabric #5 in position #9, right sides together. Press toward the strip and trim the ends, resulting in a rectangle. Sew medium fabric #5 in position #10, right sides together. Press toward the strip and trim the ends to make a square that measures 3 3/4" x 3 3/4".

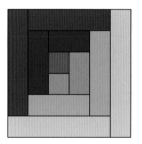

Fabric #5 added

7. Sew dark fabric #6 in position #11, right sides together. Press toward the strip and trim the ends, resulting in a rectangle. Sew dark fabric #6 in position #12, right sides together. Press toward the strip and trim the ends to make a square that measures 4 1/4" x 4 1/4".

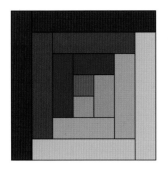

Third round of Log Cabin

8. Sew medium fabric #7 in position #13, right sides together. Press toward the strip and trim the ends, resulting in a rectangle. Sew medium fabric #7 in position #14, right sides together. Press toward the strip and trim the ends to make a square that measures 4³/4" x 4³/4".

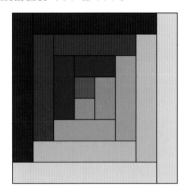

Fabric #7 added

9. Sew dark fabric #8 in position #15, right sides together. Press toward the strip and trim the ends, resulting in a rectangle. Sew dark fabric #8 in position #16, right sides together. Press toward the strip and trim the ends to make a square that measures 5¹/4" x 5¹/4".

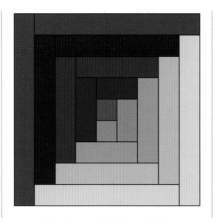

Fourth round of Log Cabin

10. Repeat Steps 1 through 9 to make the other 5 Log Cabin blocks.

Assemble the Quilt Top

LOG CABIN BLOCKS

1. Arrange the Log Cabin blocks to make 2 rows of 3 blocks. The direction of the dark and light sides of the blocks makes a field-and-furrows design.

Arrange blocks.

2. Sew the blocks to make 2 horizontal rows. Press the seams open.

3. Pin and sew row 1 to row 2, matching the seam intersections. Press this seam open.

4. The quilt top should measure 10" x 14³/4".

DOGTOOTH BORDER

1. Sort the red and tan fabrics into 2 stacks—1 with red triangles and 1 with tan triangles. Be sure the arrow notations on the triangles in each stack are pointing up. Turn the tan stack 180° to point down.

2. Sew the triangles together to form a long row, matching the alternate end and side points at the seamline. Press the seams in one direction.

TRIANGLE BORDER

In the following steps, when you place the triangle border across the quilt top, note where the triangle seams fall. Slide the border so that the triangle seams don't fall on the edge of the quilt top. This should eliminate some of the bulk of the fabric layers.

3. Place the triangle border across a short end of the Log Cabin center, with the tan triangle edge to the outside. Sew and press toward the center. Use your rotary cutter and ruler to trim the border ends even with the sides of the quilt top.

4. Place the triangle border across the adjacent long side of the quilt. Sew and press toward the center. Use your rotary cutter and ruler to trim the 2 border ends even with the sides of the quilt top.

5. Repeat Steps 3 through 4 for the third and fourth borders.

Finish the Quilt

1. Layer the backing, batting, and quilt top. Baste.

2. Quilt as desired, or follow the Suggested Quilting Design.

3. Bind. (Refer to Single-Thickness Binding on pages 17–19.)

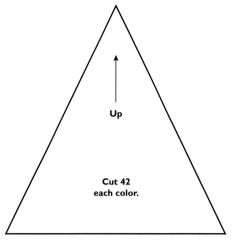

Triangle template for Dogtooth border

SUGGESTED QUILTING DESIGN

Refer to page 14 for thread suggestions.

1. Quilt each block in concentric squares, approximately ⅛" from the ditch so your stitches are visible. You will have double quilting lines approximately ¼" apart where the blocks are joined. With practice, you can eyeball all these quilting lines.

2. Quilt the Dogtooth border in-the-ditch.

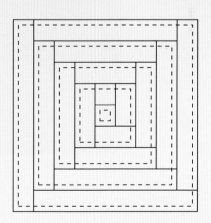

Log Cabin block quilting

Courthouse Steps with Stars

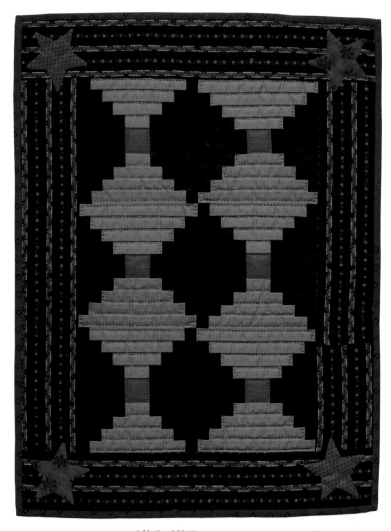

FINISHED QUILT SIZE: 15½" x 20½"   FINISHED BLOCK SIZE: 5" x 5"

This Plain Jane quilt, which enhances rather than competes with other elements of its setting, is a small rendition of a bed-sized quilt I found in a magazine. Because a Courthouse Steps or Log Cabin quilt can fool the eye about how it was pieced, I like to search for the key to the pattern.

Notice that one border is seamed together, and the design is not matched at the seam. I did this on purpose to add interest. The appliquéd stars in the corners,

which I added later, became an important design element in the success of this charming small quilt.

This small quilt has two different block piecing sequences to achieve the jagged steps in the blocks. If the blocks followed only one piecing sequence (all six blocks pieced the same), there would be double logs forming blunt ends when the blocks were joined together. You can check it out after piecing the three blocks of each set. You will like this version much better.

Fabrics

Red solid: 1 piece no smaller than 4" x 4" for block centers

Black solid: fat quarter for Courthouse Steps blocks

Tan solid: fat quarter for Courthouse Steps blocks

Black and tan stripe: fat quarter for border

Red prints: 2 different prints from pieces no smaller than 3" x 6" for the stars

Dark red print: fat quarter for single-thickness binding

Homespun plaid: ½ yard for backing

Batting: 18" x 23"

Cutting

Stars

From the red print fabrics:
Make the star template (using the template pattern on page 55) from template plastic or use your favorite appliqué method. Trace around the template to create the turning line for your needle-turn appliqué.

❋ Cut 4 stars from the 2 red fabrics, adding a fat ⅛" turn-under allowance for the needleturn appliqué.

From the black solid fabric:
❋ Cut 12 strips 1" x 18" for Courthouse Steps blocks.

From the tan solid fabric:
❋ Cut 12 strips 1" x 18" for Courthouse Steps blocks.

From the red solid fabric:
❋ Cut 6 squares 1½" x 1½" for block centers.

Border

From the black and tan stripe fabric:
❋ Cut 5 lengthwise strips 3½" x 15½".

Seam together 2 strips. Make sure the stripe pattern does not match up (refer to the color photograph). Recut this long strip to measure 15½", positioning the seam about 5" from an end.

Binding

From the dark red print fabric:
❋ Cut 4 strips 1⅛" x 22" (cut crosswise to take advantage of the slight give) for single-thickness binding. (Refer to Single-Thickness Binding on pages 17–19.)

PIECING SEQUENCE

There are two piecing sequences to make the Courthouse Steps blocks in this quilt. You will make three of each piecing sequence.

Make the Blocks

BLOCK 1

1. Sew a tan strip to opposite sides of a red $1\frac{1}{2}$" x $1\frac{1}{2}$" center square. Press to the outer edge. Use a ruler and your rotary cutter to square off the ends even with the red center. Your unit should measure $1\frac{1}{2}$" x $2\frac{1}{2}$".

2. Sew a black strip to opposite sides of the unit. Press to the outer edge. Use a ruler and your rotary cutter to square off the ends even with the tan edges. Your unit should measure $2\frac{1}{2}$" x $2\frac{1}{2}$".

3. Sew a tan strip to opposite sides of the unit. Press to the outer edge. Use a ruler and your rotary cutter to square off the ends even with the black edges. Your unit should measure $2\frac{1}{2}$" x $3\frac{1}{2}$".

4. Sew a black strip to opposite sides of the unit. Press to the outer edge. Use a ruler and your rotary cutter to square off the ends even with the tan edges. Your unit should measure $3\frac{1}{2}$" x $3\frac{1}{2}$".

5. Continue sewing in this manner until you have 4 rounds around the red center square.

6. Repeat to make 3 blocks $5\frac{1}{2}$" x $5\frac{1}{2}$".

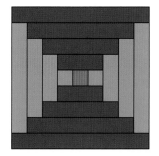

Block 1 – Courthouse Steps

BLOCK 2

1. Sew a black strip to opposite sides of a red $1\frac{1}{2}$" center square. Press to the outer edge. Use a ruler and your rotary cutter to square off the black ends even with the red center. Your unit should measure $1\frac{1}{2}$" x $2\frac{1}{2}$".

2. Sew a tan strip to opposite sides of the unit. Press to the outer edge. Use a ruler and your rotary cutter to square off the ends even with the black edges. Your unit should measure $2\frac{1}{2}$" x $2\frac{1}{2}$".

3. Sew a black strip to opposite sides of the unit. Press to the outer edge. Use a ruler and your rotary cutter to square off the ends even with the tan edges. Your unit should measure $2\frac{1}{2}$" x $3\frac{1}{2}$".

4. Sew a tan strip to opposite sides of the unit. Press to the outer edge. Use a ruler and your rotary cutter to square off the ends even with the black edges. Your unit should measure $3\frac{1}{2}$" x $3\frac{1}{2}$".

5. Continue sewing in this manner until you have 4 rounds around the red center square.

6. Repeat to make 3 blocks $5\frac{1}{2}$" x $5\frac{1}{2}$".

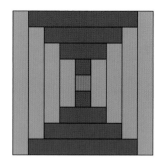

Block 2 – Courthouse Steps

Assemble the Quilt Top

COURTHOUSE STEPS BLOCKS

1. Sew the blocks to form 2 rows of 3 blocks, alternating the block sequence. This arrangement creates a neat intersection and is visually interesting. Press all the joining seams **open** to make hand quilting easier.

Sew blocks together. Press seams open.

2. Pin the first row to the second row, matching the seam intersections. Sew. Press the seam **open.** Your quilt top should measure 10½" x 15½".

BORDER

1. Pin 2 of the striped border strips to the long edges of the quilt top. Be sure 1 of the strips is the pieced border. Sew. Press toward the border.

2. Pin the remaining 2 striped border strips to the ends of the quilt top. Sew. Press toward the border.

3. Your top should measure 15½" x 20½".

Finish the Quilt

1. Layer the backing, batting, and quilt top. Baste.

2. Quilt as desired, or follow the Suggested Quilting Design.

3. Bind. (Refer to Single-Thickness Binding on pages 17–19.)

FINAL TOUCH

After you have bound the quilt, appliqué the red stars in the corners of the quilt. (Refer to Needle-turn Appliqué on pages 19–21.)

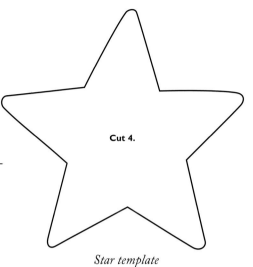

Cut 4.

Star template

SUGGESTED QUILTING DESIGN

Refer to page 14 for thread suggestions.

1. Quilt each block in concentric squares, approximately ⅛" from the ditch so your stitches are visible. You will have double quilting lines approximately ¼" apart where the blocks are joined. With practice, you can eyeball all these quilting lines.

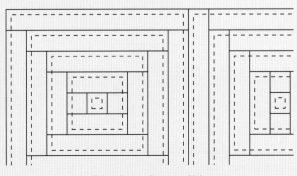

Courthouse Steps quilting

2. The border quilting is a chevron design with the "V" centered in each border. The quilting lines are approximately ¾" apart.

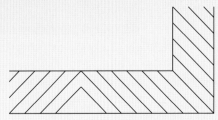

Border quilting

3. Use a ruler and a chalk wheel fabric marker to mark the border quilting design. Because chalk rubs off (which is why we use it), you must mark a line, quilt it, mark another line, quilt it, and so on.

Mini Nine-Patches
with Star Center

FINISHED QUILT SIZE: 17" x 19¼"   FINISHED BLOCK SIZE: 1⅝" x 1⅝", VARIABLE STAR 3"x 3"

The antique doll quilt that started me making a series of doll quilts using the Mini Nine-Patches had a straight block setting. After sewing dozens of small blocks, I realized that my Mini Nine-Patches consistently measured 2⅛" square, not 2" square, making them finish 1⅝" square, not 1½" square, as my math said they should measure.

I used this piecing discrepancy to my advantage in designing this doll quilt. I wanted to insert the Variable Star block in the center. Because of my slightly oversized blocks, I was able to include the tiny frame around the Star block to set it off. I made lemonade!

My piecing directions for the Mini Nine-Patches will yield three blocks from each set of fabrics, which are easier to handle than one small block. You will like these blocks so much that you will enjoy using them for other projects (such as mug mats, ornaments, pin cushions, or other small quilts—have fun!).

Follow the measurements closely for your version to go together nicely. Consistent seam allowances in your strip piecing and assembly are key in making this adorable small quilt.

Fabrics

Brown print #1: 1 piece no smaller than 4" x 4" for the Star points

Background print: 1 piece no smaller than 4" x 6" for the Star block

Dark brown check: 1 piece no smaller than 4" x 4" to frame the Star block

Various dark fabrics: 28 strips 1" x 18" for the Nine-Patches (I used 28 different dark fabrics)

Beige tone-on-tone prints: 28 assorted strips 1" x 15" from 3 or 4 different prints for the Nine-Patches

Medium red print: 3/4 yard for alternate blocks, setting triangles, and outer border

Brown print #2: fat quarter for inner border and single-thickness binding

Pink and brown print: 3/4 yard for backing

Batting: 20" x 23"

Cutting

Star Block

From the **brown print** fabric:
❋ Cut 4 squares $1^{5/8}$" x $1^{5/8}$", then cut half-square triangles for the star points. (Refer to pages 15–16 for instructions on cutting triangles.)

From the **background print** fabric:
❋ Cut 2 squares $1^{5/8}$" x $1^{5/8}$", then cut half-square triangles for the background triangles between the star points. (Refer to pages 15–16 for instructions on cutting triangles.)

❋ Cut 4 squares $1^{1/2}$" x $1^{1/2}$" for the corners of the block.

❋ Cut 1 square $1^{7/8}$" x $1^{7/8}$" for the center of the block.

From the **dark brown check** fabric:
❋ Cut 4 strips 3/4" x 4" for the Star block border.

Mini Nine-Patches

Dark fabric strips:
Recut as follows:
❋ 2 strips 1" x $6^{1/2}$"

❋ 1 strip 1" x $3^{1/2}$"

Beige tone-on-tone print strips:
Recut as follows:
❋ 1 strip 1" x $6^{1/2}$"

❋ 2 strips 1" x $3^{1/2}$"

Settings and Borders

From the **medium red print** fabric:
❋ Cut 18 squares $2^{1/8}$" x $2^{1/8}$" for alternate blocks.

❋ Cut 5 squares $3^{1/2}$" x $3^{1/2}$", then cut quarter-square triangles for setting triangles (you will have 2 extras).

❋ Cut 2 squares $2^{1/2}$" x $2^{1/2}$", then cut half-square triangles for the corners.

❋ Cut 2 strips $2^{3/8}$" x $15^{1/4}$" for the outer border.

❋ Cut 2 strips $2^{3/8}$" x $16^{3/4}$" for the outer border.

Inner Border and Binding

From the **brown print** fabric:
❋ Cut 2 strips 1" x $14^{1/4}$" for the inner border.

❋ Cut 2 strips 1" x 12" for the inner border.

❋ Cut 4 strips $1^{1/8}$" x 22" from the fat quarter for single-thickness binding. (Refer to Single-Thickness Binding on pages 17–19.)

Make the Blocks

STAR BLOCK

1. Sew the long side of a brown star point to a side of the corner square. Repeat to make 4 units. Carefully press toward the triangle.

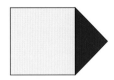

Make 4.

2. Sew the long side of a brown star point to the adjacent side of the corner square. Repeat to make 4 units. Carefully press toward the triangle.

3. Using your rotary cutter and ruler, evenly trim the corner units to measure $1^{7}/8$" along the diagonal formed by the 2 star point triangles.

Trim corner units.

4. Sew 2 background triangles to the sides of 2 corner units. Press toward the background triangle.

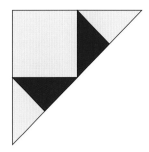

Sew background triangles to corner units.

5. Sew 2 short corner units to opposite sides of the center square. Carefully press toward the center.

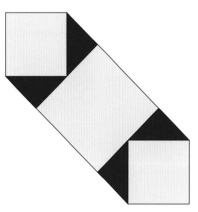

Sew short corner units to center square.

6. Pin and sew the remaining corner units to opposite sides of the center square, matching the seam intersections.

Sew remaining corner units to center square.

7. Use the Clipping Trick (refer to page 17) at all the seam intersections. Press the center part of the seam toward the center block, press the outer edge of the seam toward the background triangle, and press the seam intersections open. Repeat for all 4 intersections on the Star block.

8. Use your rotary cutter and ruler to square up the block to $3^{1}/2$" x $3^{1}/2$".

9. Sew 2 of the dark brown check strips to opposite sides of the Star block. Press toward the dark brown strips. Use your rotary cutter and ruler to trim the ends of the strips even with the Star block.

10. Sew the 2 remaining dark brown check strips to opposite sides of the Star block. Press toward the dark brown strips. Use your rotary cutter and ruler to trim the ends of the strips even with the Star block.

11. Using your rotary cutter and ruler, square the framed Star block to $3^{3}/4$" x $3^{3}/4$".

CONSISTENCY COUNTS

A consistent scant $1/4$" seam allowance is necessary, so keep checking your measurements.

MINI NINE-PATCHES

Remember that these instructions will yield three blocks from each set of fabrics, which are easier to handle than just one block.

1. Sew the long 6½" fabric strips together in a dark–light–dark sequence. Press the seams toward the dark fabric.

2. Sew the short 3½" fabric strips together in a light–dark–light sequence. Press the seams toward the dark fabric.

3. Cut the long pieced strip into 1" sections to yield 6 pieces.

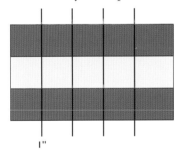

Cut 6 pieces.

4. Cut the short pieced strip into 1" sections to yield 3 pieces.

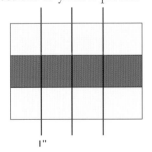

Cut 3 pieces.

5. Sew a dark–light–dark section to a light–dark–light section, matching the seam intersections.

6. Sew a dark–light–dark section to the other side of the light–dark–light section, matching the seam intersections. Press the last 2 seams **open** to eliminate some of the bulk for quilting. These units should measure 2⅛" x 2⅛" (to finish 1⅝" x 1⅝").

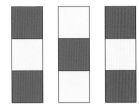

Match intersections and sew.

7. Make 28 Mini Nine-Patches for your quilt. You will also have 56 Mini Nine-Patches for other projects.

Make 28.

Assemble the Quilt Top

BLOCKS

1. Arrange the Mini Nine-Patches, the alternate blocks, and the framed Star block to make 6 rows of 5 blocks on point. Fill in with the setting block squares and the setting triangles.

Arrange blocks.

2. Sew the blocks in diagonal rows. Press the seams toward the setting blocks or triangles.

3. Pin the first row to the second row, matching the seam intersections. Sew. Use the Clipping Trick at the seam intersections. Press the seam intersections open and the remainder of the seam toward the setting blocks or triangles.

4. Join both ends of rows 5 and 6 and add the Star block in the center.

5. After you have sewn all the rows, add the corner triangles. Press toward the corners.

6. Carefully trim the excess on all 4 sides, leaving a ¼" seam allowance.

7. Your quilt top should measure 12" x 14¼".

INNER BORDER

1. Pin and sew the 2 longer inner border strips to the sides of the quilt. Press toward the border.

2. Pin and sew the 2 remaining inner border strips to the top and bottom of the quilt. Press toward the border.

OUTER BORDER

1. Pin and sew the 15¼" outer border strips to the sides of the quilt. Press toward the outer border.

2. Pin and sew the remaining outer border strips to the top and bottom of the quilt. Press toward the outer border.

Finish the Quilt

1. Layer the backing, batting, and quilt top. Baste.

2. Quilt as desired, or follow the Suggested Quilting Design.

3. Bind. (Refer to Single-Thickness Binding on pages 17–19.)

SUGGESTED QUILTING DESIGN

Refer to page 14 for thread suggestions.

1. Quilt the Star block seams in-the-ditch.

2. Quilt the outside edge of the Star block in-the-ditch.

3. Carefully quilt the narrow dark brown frame in-the-ditch.

4. Quilt an X across each Mini Nine-Patch block, using a continuous line from the inside edge of the inner border to the opposite inside edge of the inner border.

5. Quilt in-the-ditch next to the inside of the inner border.

6. Quilt about ⅛" from the outside edge of the inner border.

7. Quilt an X in each setting block, as you did for the Mini Nine-Patch blocks. This creates a grid over the center of the quilt.

8. I used a diagonal crosshatch grid to quilt the outer border. Establish the first set of lines using a ruler. Line it up with the Mini Nine-Patch blocks on point. Using a chalk wheel marker with the ruler as a guide, draw the line. Quilt the line. Proceed in this manner to get a large crosshatch grid on the outer border.

9. Create another grid between the first quilted lines. This will create a grid of quilting lines about ¾" apart, which makes a nice scale for this adorable small quilt.

Quilting design

About the Author

About the Auth

Jo Morton was introduced to quilting in 1979 and hasn't put down her needle since. She began teaching quiltmaking in 1982 and in 1985 started to create small quilts with the charm of antiques, or "new quilts that look old."

Jo has sold her small quilts since 1988 and has traveled East to exhibit at juried folk-art shows in Ohio, Pennsylvania, Virginia, and New England. She has made commissioned and custom-framed small quilts. Jo's quilts have been listed in the *Early American Life Directory of American Traditional Crafts from 1990 to 2002.*

Jo's quilts have been featured in *American Patchwork & Quilting, Quilter's Newsletter Magazine, Early American Life, Miniature Quilts, Ladies Circle Patchwork Quilts,* and *Country Business.* She also creates fabric lines for Andover Fabrics.

Jo lives in Nebraska City with her husband, Russ, and two cats.

Photo by Mark Jewell

Index

Photo by Mark Jewell

Photo by Mark Jewell

C&T booklist

15 Two-Block Quilts: Unlock the Secrets of Secondary Patterns, Claudia Olson

24 Quilted Gems: Sparkling Traditional & Original Projects, Gai Perry

All About Quilting from A to Z, From the Editors and Contributors of Quilter's Newsletter Magazine and Quiltmaker Magazine

America's Printed Fabrics 1770—1890: 8 Reproduction Quilt Projects •Hitoric Notes & Photographs • Dating Your Quilts, Barbara Brackman

An Amish Adventure, 2nd Edition: A Workbook for Color in Quilts, Roberta Horton

Appliqué 12 Easy Ways!: Charming Quilts, Giftable Projects & Timeless Techniques, Elly Sienkiewicz

Appliqué Delights: 100 Irresistible Blocks from Piece O' Cake Designs, Becky Goldsmith & Linda Jenkins

Appliqué Inside the Lines: 12 Quilt Projects to Embroider & Appliqué, Carol Armstrong

Art of Classic Quiltmaking, The, Harriet Hargrave & Sharyn Craig

Art of Machine Piecing, The: How to Achieve Quality Workmanship Through a Colorful Journey, Sally Collins

At Piece With Time: A Woman's Journey Stitched in Cloth, Kristin Steiner & Diane Frankenberger

Beading Basics: 30 Embellishing Techniques for Quilters, Mary Stori

Beautifully Quilted with Alex Anderson: • How to Choose or Create the Best Designs for Your Quilt • 5 Timeless Projects • Full-size Patterns, Ready to Use, Alex Anderson

Benni Harper's Quilt Album: A Scrapbook of Quilt Projects, Photos & Never-Before-Told Stories, Earlene Fowler & Margrit Hall

Best of Baltimore Beauties, The: 95 Patterns for Album Blocks and Borders, Elly Sienkiewicz

Block Magic, Too!: Over 50 NEW Blocks from Squares and Rectangles, Nancy Johnson-Srebro

Borders, Bindings & Edges: The Art of Finishing Your Quilt, Sally Collins

Celebrate Great Quilts! circa 1820—1940: The International Quilt Festival Collection, Karey Patterson Bresenhan & Nancy O'Bryant

Celebrate the Tradition with C&T Publishing: Over 70 Fabulous New Blocks, Tips & Stories from Quilting's Best, C&T Staff

Circle Play: Simple Designs for Fabulous Fabrics, Reynola Pakusich

Classic Four-Block Appliqué Quilts: A Back-to-Basics Approach, Gwen Marston

Color Play: Easy Steps to Imaginative Color in Quilts, Joen Wolfrom

Country Quilts for Friends: 18 Charming Projects for All Seasons, Margaret Peters & Anne Sutton

Crazy Quilt Handbook, The: Revised, 2nd Edition, Judith Baker Montano

Curl-Up Quilts: Flannel Appliqué & More from Piece O' Cake Designs, Becky Goldsmith & Linda Jenkins

Diamond Quilts & Beyond: From the Basics to Dazzling Designs, Jan Krentz

Dolls of the Art Deco Era 1910—1940: Collect, Restore, Create & Play, Susanna Oroyan

Easy Chennille Appliqué: Create Dimension the Color Stick Way, Cheryl Malkowski

Elm Creek Quilts: Quilt Projects Inspired by the Elm Creek Quilts Novels, Jennifer Chiaverini & Nancy Odom

Enchanted Views: Quilts Inspired by Wrought-Iron Designs, Dilys Fronks

Fantastic Fabric Folding: Innovative Quilting Projects, Rebecca Wat

Fantastic Fans: Exquisite Quilts & Other Projects, Alice Dunsdon

Fast, Fun & Easy Fabric Bags: 10 Projects to Suit Your Style, Pam Archer

Fast, Fun & Easy Irresist-a-Bowls: 5 Fresh New Projects, You Can't Make Just One, Linda Johansen

Fast, Fun & Easy Fabric Knitting: Fabulous Projects–Great New Looks, Cyndy Lyle Rymer

Felt Wee Folk: Enchanting Projects, Salley Mavor

Finish It with Alex Anderson: 6 Quilt Projects • Choose the Perfect Border • Options for Edges, Alex Anderson

Floral Affair, A: Quilts & Accessories for Romantics, Nihon Vogue

Four Seasons in Flannel: 23 Projects—Quilts & More, Jean Wells & Lawry Thorn

From the Cover: 15 Memorable Projects for Quilt Lovers, Mary Leman Austin & Quilter's Newsletter Magazine Editors & Contributors

Gathered Garden, A: 3-Dimensional Fabric Flowers •15 Projects–Quilts & More •Mix & Match Bouquets, Carol Armstrong

Get Creative with M'Liss Rae Hawley: A Beginner's Guide to Color & Design for Quilters, M'liss Rae Hawley

Hand Quilting with Alex Anderson: Six Projects for First-Time Hand Quilters, Alex Anderson

Heirloom Machine Quilting, 4rd Edition: Comprehensive Guide to Hand-Quilting Effects Using Your Sewing Machine, Harriet Hargrave

Hidden Block Quilts: • Discover New Blocks Inside Traditional Favorites • 13 Quilt Settings • Instructions for 76 Blocks, Lerlene Nevaril

Hunter Star Quilts & Beyond: Techniques & Projects with Infinite Possibilities, Jan Krentz

Keep Quilting with Alex Anderson: 7 Skill-Building Piecing Techniques • 16 traditional blocks to Mix & Match •6 Sampler Star Projects, Alex Anderson

Kids Start Quilting with Alex Anderson: •7 Fun & Easy Projects •Quilts for Kids by Kids • Tips for Quilting with Children, Alex Anderson

Laurel Burch Christmas, A: Color the Season Beautiful with 25 Quilts & Crafts, Laurel Burch

FOR MORE INFORMATION

Ask for a free catalog:

C&T Publishing, Inc. • P.O. Box 1456 • Lafayette, CA 94549 • 800-284-1114

email: ctinfo@ctpub.com • website: www.ctpub.com

QUILTING SUPPLIES

Cotton Patch Mail Order • 3404 Hall Lane • Dept. CTB • Lafayette, CA 94549 • 800-835-4418 • 925-283-7883

email: quiltusa@yahoo.com • website: www.quiltusa.com

Note: Fabrics used in the quilts shown may not be currently available because fabric manufacturers keep most fabrics in print for only a short time.